Musings By Mo

MAUREEN CRAIG MCINTOSH

Paperback ISBN: 978-0-9686614-2-0
ePub ISBN: 978-0-9686614-3-7
mobi ISBN: 978-0-9686614-4-4

Written by Maureen Craig McIntosh
Cover by Axion Marketing
Edited by Marlene Oulton
Published by Cheeky Kea Printworks

Edition Number 1.00

DEDICATION

I want to dedicate this book to two of the most important mentors in my life to date. First, Dr. William Glasser, who was my friend, mentor, and teacher for over twenty-eight years, and second, Christian Simpson, who as my present coach and mentor has inspired me to write my daily musings which make up this book. I thank both of these men for their invaluable teachings and for the awareness they have brought into my life.

I would also like to say a special thank you to the members of my Inner Circle who have shared their gratitude with me many times over for sending out my daily writings. I appreciate your kindness in sharing how my thoughts have caused you pause and consider areas of your own life that can be changed for the better.

To my son Shawn, his wonderful wife Olga, my grandchildren Nicholas, Peter, Ansley, and to my lovely step-daughter, Megan, her husband Dave, and son Dylan, I thank you for being in my world. I cherish each call, hug, or smile I receive from all of you. Know that some of my greatest learning has come from my grandchildren.

Lastly, and certainly not the least by any means, I would like to thank my partner, Doug. You are always so supportive of me and my goals, and often see in me what sometimes I do not see in myself. Your presence in my life brings me unparalleled happiness and for that I am truly grateful.

FOREWORD

When people learn Choice Theory, it seems to have a profound impact on their lives. In *Mo's Musings*, Maureen McIntosh teaches Choice Theory in a profoundly creative way. She has taught Dr. William Glasser's ideas for many years and thousands of people have been touched by her warm and friendly approach to teaching, but this little book encapsulates these ideas in a subtle delivery system which is very effective as well as entertaining. This book allows the reader to eavesdrop on the random musings of an excellent and caring mentor.

In each musing, Maureen tells a little story from her own life experiences. At the end of each one she asks readers some questions to help them internalize the concepts and determine how to use the ideas to add value to their own lives.

When I opened to a random page in her book, I found one called "Retirement." In it she says, "There is always one thing in life we can be sure of and that is change." The questions she asks the reader at the end are, "Do you think about retirement? Do you have a plan?"

There is a lot of Choice Theory embodied in those two questions. Thinking and acting are the only components of our behavior that we can control. Focusing on what we are doing, essentially the choices we are making in life, has the most likely chance of getting us what we want.

Mo's Musings is filled with ideas that everyone can use to discover what they need to be happy. Read one a day and see how you can change your life for the better.

Carleen Glasser, MA, CTRTC, author of *Thoughtful Answers to Timeless Questions*, www.WGlasserBooks.com.

Introduction

In this book you will find 90 of my daily writings that I send out via email to my Inner Circle. This process would not have happened if I had not learned about e-mail marketing from my mentor and coach, Christian Simpson.

These daily musings were designed to entertain and add value to my coaching clients, and now I hope they will add value to your life via this book.

These musings have been written from my lifetime of learning and growing across various stages of my life, but particularly my journey with the late Dr. William Glasser, founder of Reality Therapy and Choice Theory. One of the most powerful contributions made by Dr. Glasser was the art of self-evaluation in the Reality Therapy Communication Process, and in each of these I hope to make the reader take pause and think about some aspect of their life.

In the majority of these pages you will find some questions that will help you to think into your own situation and evaluate for yourself what you would want or do.

You do not need to read this book all at once. Just let the book open naturally, pick a page, and see how it speaks to you that day.

I truly hope that in some small or big way these musings will add value to your life.

Yours in growing awareness,

Maureen Craig Mc Intosh

1 Crow Sorrow...

"1 crow sorrow, 2 crows joy, 3 crows a letter, 4 crows a boy, 5 crows silver, 6 crows gold, 7 crows a secret that should never be told."

Today, while driving to visit my son, his wife, and grandchildren, I saw six crows on a hydro wire and remembered the rhyme I've written here. This is a rhyme that my mother recited every time she saw crows. I suddenly became aware that this is a perfect example of how beliefs in the way of superstitions can creep into our subconscious and we are totally unaware of that happening.

Imagine seeing one crow and telling yourself you will have sorrow! This message goes into the universe immediately, and the next thing you know something happens and you feel the sorrow. Oh, how right that superstition becomes at that moment!

Is this not ridiculous? There are many other sayings like "Don't step on a crack, you will break your mother's back" or if someone buys you a set of knives, it is bad luck unless you pay the person a cent. Also, let's not forget the very famous one that says "Don't walk under a ladder or you will have bad luck." How about this one: "Don't sit on the table. You will be married before you are able!"

Imagine the effect on the behaviors one chooses when reciting these superstitions. Could they be limiting us in our day-to-day activity? Do they interfere with your thinking?

Do you hold on to superstitions? If so, how do they limit you?

While watching Downton Abbey, they were talking about how the groom cannot see the bride the day before the wedding as it would bring bad luck! Is this really true? Are we lead to believe that?

Maybe I am the oddball here, having grown up hearing all these superstitions. However, I do know that we definitely need to be mindful of all the crazy things we learn and separate fact from fiction!

SPEAKING ENGAGEMENT

In 1984, a co-worker and I had our first speaking engagement to parents at a local elementary school. I, for one, was terrified, but my co-worker was an extrovert so she worked diligently preparing all the information. All I had to do was organize it and get ready to deliver the talk.

Looking back, I almost laugh out loud. In fact, she and I have many laughs over that first speaking engagement. Neither one of us ever thought we would speak in public, let alone talk about sex. We were both very nervous! The District Medical Health Officer gave us one piece of advice I have never forgotten. He said "Remember you are being asked to speak because you are perceived as the experts in the subject area, and you need to tell yourselves you are the experts because it's true!" Without missing a beat, we became the experts.

We arrived at the elementary school to find sixty parents sitting in the auditorium staring at us. We had a small lectern that we were both fighting over. We were so nervous that our knees were literally knocking together. How would they receive what we are about to say? How would they treat us? Would they throw us out? What would they say when we tell them their children are sexual beings right from birth? These were all things we were learning and about to share with them.

At the end of that first speaking engagement, we received a standing ovation! People rushed to the front of the room. They were so grateful that finally someone was willing to discuss this important issue! We were overwhelmed with their gratitude and at the same we walked out of that school on the biggest high ever! It was like we were walking on a cloud.

Today I can look back at that event and see it as a time when I really stepped out of my comfort zone for the betterment of myself. The whole purpose was to add value to the parent's knowledge base, but I know I received a valuable lesson as well. When you help someone else, then they want to help you! We were invited to nearly every Home and School meeting for the rest of that year. We spoke 110 times and got pretty comfortable with our subject material and speaking in public. It is really funny to me how we would make a bold statement, then say "Okay?" and get away with it.

We were successful, not so much because of our speaking skills, but because we were willing to talk about a taboo subject; a subject which so many people had so many questions about. We soon became very need satisfying. We built a solid relationship with the adults in the community as we met their needs and they trusted us! We discovered that this was key to our success in working with the youth.

What are you currently challenged by? Are you facing it head on or shrinking away from it? What happens in either case? There are so many comfort zones in one's lifetime that have to be broken through. Are you breaking any comfort zones these days?

A Bad Week

Recently I worked with someone who told me he had a bad week. As we were talking he had difficulty explaining why he felt that way. His relationships were good, his wife and sons are happy and his friends were well. The only thing he could think of was that his baseball season was over. As we continued talking he realized that it was not the baseball he missed as much as the friendships he had made with the team members.

As we continued talking I asked him what he wanted in his life. He had a hard time to articulate anything other than a specific type of house he would like to have. He followed that immediately with "I know I will never get that so why bother dreaming about it!"

The more we talked, the more he realized that he could not see beyond his own current state of affairs, and that he continued to go around and around in circles chasing a goal.

As a man in his mid-forties, he told me he has no dreams, nothing he aspired to do. I discovered that he had an elderly member of his family that was very demanding and draining of his time and energy.

The more we talked, the more he revealed that he had spent his life giving to everyone else and that he was feeling burnt out. We talked a lot about the need to fill ourselves up, to take care of ourselves first because if we do not, we will have nothing to give to others.

You see, he was seeing himself as this unworthy person who through his burn out, had nothing left to give. He could not even allow himself to dream. When work is demanding, home is demanding, and you are demanding of yourself, what can only happen is burn out!

He had pictures in his mind of himself being more physically fit, eating healthier, and exercising regularly, but felt badly when he didn't do it. So much so that he no longer allowed himself to dream. He suggested that he did not know how to dream or what to wish for. Yes, he was depressed and looking for a solution.

He realized that the only thing he could do is choose to take charge of his life! The biggest thing for him was having no dreams. I told him that the next week he was to focus on what made him cry, what made him laugh, and when these things happened, did he have a tendency to let his mind wander. His dreams and purpose could be right there.

Do you dream? What do you cry about? What do you laugh about? Pay attention to your thoughts as they might surprise you.

A Birthday

When my grandson turned eight, it was wonderful to be able to drive down the road and join him to celebrate his birthday. His gift from me was a very old fashioned game of croquet. At first when he opened it he had a sad look on his face because he did not know what it was or how to play it. I asked him if he was feeling unwell. He replied no and that he was okay.

Then suddenly he said "Can we take this outside and play with it right now?" and we all said yes. We went outdoors, set the game up, and talked about how we were going to play it for the first time. He and his brother, sister, and mother, all learned how to play at least a little.

After awhile, he looked at me and said "Grammy, this is an awesome gift! Thank you. Mama always wants me to play outside, but I tell her I don't want to because there is nothing to do. It is boring outside. Now I have something I can do with everyone! We can even move it around and make it the way we want." He was so pleased.

"Phew," I thought! I was a little worried that he would be disappointed, but really felt that he would enjoy it once he got the hang of it. Regardless of that, I am very proud of his parents. He would never say he did not like something because after all, it was a gift. He graciously accepted it before he understood what it was all about.

We really enjoyed our time with him and the family. As a friend said on my Facebook page, there is nothing like grandchildren to help us be young again. At one point I told the kids my back was sore and the middle one who is five said, "Grammy, I know what to do. Come with me." I followed him and he showed me a low to the ground wooden lawn chair. He said, "Sit sideways and then turn around." I said I might never get up again to which he replied, "Don't worry Gram, I will help you up, but right now rest your back." So cute to hear advice coming out of a five-year-old's mouth.

You can see these children bring a lot of joy into my life! Let me ask you –what brings *you* joy?

A Fun Week

Recently I had a really fun week. What more could Grammy Mo ask for than to spend time with three of her grandchildren, right? For two nights I got to sleep at their house because Papa was away for work and Mom wanted some help, especially in the evening.

To top things off, I had a great time with some of my favorite girlfriends this afternoon and they loaded me up with toys for the little ones! Guess who the happy campers were?

That's right – Mom, Grammy, and the kids! We had a lot of fun putting together puzzles, reading stories, and just talking about ancient times when Grammy Mo was a little girl!

Children are such a joy. They are full of curiosity and really just want to know the why and how of everything. Each one of them has their own talents and they automatically are drawn to where their natural interests lie.

At a certain point, my daughter-in-law looked at me and said, "I think we all have a little bit of a child in us!" I laughed and agreed, but replied, "How many of us forget to tap into our inner child?" You see, your inner child does not worry about what people think; they are naturally curious, explorers, and story tellers.

How do we lose all that as we grow up? Think about the adults in your life when you were a child. What were some of the stories that they told you? What were some of the beliefs they offered you that you willingly took on just because these people were important to you?

I am working hard to be a consciously aware grandparent and choose very carefully how I want to influence my grandchildren. We are all at different stages in life and we had a discussion about classic books and how well they were written in the language of the day. Then I came across a sentence in a story that referred to some kids as stupid! Did I really want to share that wording? Of course I didn't! We are evolving ever so slowly as a society, but when we catch ourselves making a mistake and do an immediate course correction, it feels good.

I don't know why I am writing all of this down, but maybe there is just a little food for thought in these few words. It has been a real blast spending more time with the little ones who are, shall I say, "real." They are truly getting real with Grammy Mo!

A Precocious Young Man

I used to work with the school counselors at the middle and the high school level. One day I received a call from the school counselor in a k-8 school who told me he was beside himself with frustration.

He shared that he had been working with a nine-year-old little boy at school. This boy was continually getting in trouble for grabbing at the girls. He would pinch their buttocks or try to grab their breasts. The counselor was very concerned that maybe he was or had been in a sexually abusive situation.

We were only working with twelve to twenty-five-year-olds at that time, but I agreed to see this child. I really did not know what I was going to do, but after talking with him I decided to show him a video for boys about body changes. Nine years old was a little young to talk about sex back in those days, but I showed him the video anyway.

It explained all about puberty and the changes our body goes through when entering this stage and adolescence. At the end of the video, he looked at me, his mother, and the counselor, put his arm in the air and pulled up his shirt. He said, "Did that movie mean 'hair' like this?" He had a large growth of underarm hair and said he had pubic hair as well. He had been bathing himself for a long time so his mother had no idea that he was going through these bodily changes.

To be developed to that stage at such a young age is very rare for a boy. He was what we would describe as precocious in his development. We had a long talk about all he was experiencing and feeling. He felt really good as he realized he was normal. He was also open to learning that the behaviors he was choosing were not appropriate.

I believe that early development may be happening more often today due to all the hormones and chemicals that are in our food, and I advocate for eating free range meats, eggs, etc. to avoid excessive intake of unnatural additives.

All behavior is purposeful and for this little boy, he was doing the best he could do with the strong biological urges he was feeling! Once he got new information and was taught how to deal with his feelings, including masturbation, he never misbehaved in school again.

Abundance Or Lack?

Today I had a coaching conversation with someone who was complaining about how there is a lack of money in her life. This person was saying that there is always a feeling of lack in the financial department. As a coach, I understand that the client has all the answers within them and that I need to get really curious.

I've worked with Julie now for a year or so. She gets just so much money and then the "lack" sets in. I am seeing a pattern so I asked her three simple questions.

1. *Are you comfortable in this situation because you have known this most of your life and you know how to deal with it?*

She said they had never really thought about that. It is like the Law of Attraction. We attract what we are comfortable with or what we know. This is why we will never advance in our careers or in making money because we keep attracting the same type of situations into our lives. It is what we have always known.

So I moved on to the next question.

2. *Do you think you are really opening yourself up to abundance?*

Again, another question with a different twist and perspective. I was really curious and I wondered if this was so. I recognized that there was always an excuse why she could not do something that could potentially bring in more clients. Julie could not accept the possibility of abundance because she had never experienced it. You see, as a child there was never enough to go around. There was always this perceived "lack" in her household. Her family constantly struggled to find the next bit of money and it produced a high stress environment.

So I became even more curious and moved to the next question.

3. *Is it serving you somehow to always create this level of stress and are you addicted to the perceived "lack" and the chemical effect the stress offers you?*

This question really floored her. She wanted to dig deeper. She had never thought of it this way, but it is like any addiction which triggers a chemical reaction in the body. We become addicted to the sensation whether positive or negative. She could feel the shift inside of her and realized she needed to think more deeply about these questions. Could it be they were true? She realized she was limiting herself and it came down to her own thinking about scarcity and abundance.

What do you think? Do you have a scarcity mindset or an abundance mindset? How does either of them serve you?

Ageless Goddess

I have followed Dr. Christiane Northrup for the last twenty plus years. She is an obstetrician, gynecologist from Yarmouth, Maine, which is not too far from here. She wrote the book *The Wisdom of Menopause*, updated it in 2012, and it is one of the best books I have read about the subject. She not only talks about the medical approach, but is well versed on the alternative approaches for women's health. She is Oprah's gynecologist.

She recently released a new book geared toward women over fifty. It is called the *Ageless Goddess*. Even if you are not a woman in this age bracket there is some very important information in her book about how to take personal responsibility for our own health. She is taking us down a path of a different way of thinking! She says:

> *"Growing older is an opportunity for you to increase your value and competence as the neural connections in your hippocampus and throughout your brain increase, weaving into your brain and body the wisdom of a life well lived, which allows you to stop living out of fear or disappointing others and being imperfect. Ageless living is courageous living. It means being undistracted by the petty dramas of life because you have enough experience to know what's not worth worrying about and what ought to be your priorities. It means establishing a new relationship to time, where you stop fearing it or trying to out run it. When people over 100 were asked in a recent interview, how they felt about reaching the triple digits, the top three answers were 'blessed', 'happy' and surprised because when you're living agelessly, you don't pay attention to your age, whatever it is."*

Unfortunately, Northrup says we often forget about this in the onslaught of ageist cultural messages. We need to be more aware of our culture's negative messages about growing older and make a conscious effort to reject them.

Think about this message. Whether you are twenty, thirty, forty, fifty, or sixty and over, there is some wisdom for us all since we are all growing older! When she talks about a life well lived, we create that in our younger years!

She talks about ageless living. I have heard thirty-year-olds worrying about being old! I think we could all learn to live agelessly if we chose to live in the present.

So what about our relationship with time?

I often hear things like "If I ever have time I'll..." or "I am so busy, there isn't enough time in the day." Could we not all develop a different relationship to our time and learn to manage it rather than it managing us?

Once again we are challenged to become more consciously aware of those ageist messages that we are telling ourselves and make an effort to reject them.

What say you? Will you drop those ageist messages that you give yourself or continue to buy into them?

Reunions

Awhile back I had the wonderful opportunity to gather together with nine of my fifteen former nursing school classmates. The last time we were all together was thirty-five years ago. We graduated in 1969 and hadn't gotten together since our ten year reunion.

When receiving the invitation my initial question was "Why a reunion now?" Life gets busy and we all have great intentions, but nurses in particular spend a lot of time looking after everyone else but themselves. They are givers – just as you are. So why wait so long before having a reunion?

I pondered this today. We have all had amazing life journeys: some tragedies along the way, some failed relationships, but mostly we have had a great life! We have lost two of our fifteen classmates over the years due to illness so the rest of us are feeling blessed.

One person was supposed to join us, but she found out she had a loose wheel on her car! Why did this happen? Do you ever question the reason for things such as this happening? We were all looking so forward to seeing this person, but alas it was not to be.

Do you question events in your life? Or are you like most people, just floating along in your business? Did you know that we live 72-93% of our day in our subconscious mind? Think about that. We get up, get dressed, make breakfast, get in our car, and even drive to work, all subconsciously. Have you ever stopped and brought your behavior into your conscious awareness?

Dr. Glasser gave us the best gift of all in teaching us about Total Behavior in his book *Choice Theory, 1998*. He taught that "All behavior is purposeful" and that all behavior is designed to get us something that we want. In the end it will satisfy one or more of our basic needs.

Total behavior has four parts to it.

FEELING
PHYSIOLOGY
THINKING
ACTING

As I write this I think about our reunion. We laughed our heads off as nurses as we talked about our group's combined physical ailments. Happily, nearly everyone in the group did not let their emotions take over with these elements and have taken control to do something about their maladies. This was a positive thing because do you know what happens when we become emotionally overwhelmed? We have no direct control over our feelings and physiology, but we do have control over our thinking and acting.

What I love about learning total behavior is that we can learn to deal with our emotions and body talk which are designed to keep us behaving, and bring them into our conscious awareness where we can check our thinking and acting. You see, our total behavior happens so rapidly in our subconscious mind, but what happens when you train your mind to become more consciously aware? Think about it. Do you have more or less control over your life?

What a gift we have been given by Dr. William Glasser to be able to understand how to become more consciously aware.

BEING A GOOD LISTENER

Are you a good listener? Do you have a communication process?

I want to talk a little about the procedures that lead to change or the Reality Therapy Communication Process. So what are these procedures you may wonder?

What is really important is to create a relationship with the person you are interacting with. Some would say create the counseling environment, but I see it as creating a relationship with everyone you deal with on a regular basis. Regardless of who that person is, you are deciding how you want to relate to them. This is a communication process that works regardless of the situation.

Listen with a caring ear. Listen to hear what the person is saying. It is not listening if you are planning your next statement while they are still speaking. Think about the other person's basic needs. What need could they potentially be trying to satisfy?

Find out what the person really wants.

For example, I often have people tell me that they have just been attacked verbally by their partner or child, or they themselves have done this and then they do not feel well emotionally. When someone loses it, what is it that they really want? The issue at hand is not always the issue: It may be something else altogether. Maybe they are upset over a financial issue and get upset about it when in reality what they really want is some attention, but they do not have the communication skills to express what they really want, which is love and belonging?

Find out what they have been doing to get what they really want.

Ask them to evaluate that behavior. For example, is complaining about finances getting you what you really want, which is more time with a loved one? We need to be very careful when asking someone to evaluate their behavior. They need to feel like they can trust us and that they have a good relationship with us. Otherwise, it may backfire on you.

Figure out if you can come up with a plan to work things out so you both get more of what you want.

BET ON YOURSELF

This week I decided to continue to work on the John Maxwell Team online university. Thinking about my own growth and goals I decided to start with the *15 Invaluable Laws of Growth*, a program I sometimes teach.

As I was listening to John Maxwell he spoke about the self-image lid. He went on to say the most important person you listen to daily is yourself.

What kinds of things do you say to yourself daily? Are you even aware of those self-imposed messages?

There are four things you can do daily to lift your self-image lid:

GUARD YOUR SELF-TALK
ADD VALUE TO OTHERS
DO THE RIGHT THING EVEN WHEN IT IS HARD
EVERYDAY GET A WIN.

GUARD YOUR SELF-TALK
Become more self-aware of those messages we give ourselves. Stop and ask yourself if it is true before you speak it.

ADD VALUE TO OTHERS
It is impossible to feel bad about yourself when you are helping others.

DO THE RIGHT THING EVEN WHEN IT IS HARD
This is a big one because it is about what you value. Whenever, we go against what we value there is only one person we hurt and that is ourselves.

EVERYDAY GET A WIN
Ask yourself, what am I going to do today to give me my win? Figure out what you need to do to feel better about yourself.

Here's the thing. Why would anyone else bet on you if you are not willing to bet on yourself?

CHALLENGES OR OPPORTUNITIES

While on vacation heading to Orlando, we decided to move to the Silver Lake Resort Hotel. This was something I had taken a chance on reserving sight unseen and didn't know much about the location.

Someone gave me an address to buy resort certificates. I had never done anything like this in my life, but I decided to try it out. I bought $400.00 worth of certificates for which I was charged on my credit card. Then when I booked the resort to use the certificate I was charged another $361.00. I could not figure out why.

When we arrived at the resort we discovered it was a beautiful location! We could see why we were charged more. In the end we stayed at a resort that had everything we could possibly want for $761 for seven nights. Not bad for Florida considering that we were going to pay $1295.00 at the hotel where the conference was located.

We were surprised though when we realized that our room would not be tended unless we asked it to be. We were provided with garbage bags and were invited to take them to the trash area once they were full. We were given enough towels, toilet paper, etc. for the entire week and were on our own to make our bed.

Initially I thought, "Wow, this is not cool," but the more I thought about it, the better I liked it. You see, it was like our apartment away from home. There was something reassuring about knowing that no one else would enter our room for the week. We walked by the trash area every day and really, how often do we put the trash out at our home anyway? It was an interesting and unexpected experience.

You see, things are not always as they seem. We took a risk and we adapted. The best part of it was that I could not only wash towels if I needed to, but I had access to a free laundry area to wash all of our clothes which we did do. How easily can we change our thinking to find the opportunities in every challenge no matter how big or how small?

What are your challenges today? And more importantly, where is your opportunities?

All Behavior Is Purposeful

All behavior is purposeful, so if we keep this in mind, we need to find out the purpose of the behavior of some of the people in our life. So often we make the mistake of assuming we know what their behavior means.

But there is only one way to be sure and that is to ask the person who owns the behavior for they are the only ones who know why they are doing what they are doing.

So often we see a situation and we take in the information through our senses. We attach our perspective to it and then act as if what we have just created it too, and we have never checked with the person involved to see if our assumptions are correct.

It reminds me of the woman who always wanted a dozen red roses for Valentine's Day, but she never ever got them. She would get depressed, be upset, and her husband would not be able to figure out why she was sad. She had never stated clearly what she wanted and felt let down when he didn't give her what she desired.

One day her children asked her what she would like for Valentine's Day and she told them she had always wanted a dozen red roses. They told their father and the very next Valentine's she received her roses and was very happy.

How often do we expect someone to read our mind? This is no different than perceiving something, adding our perspective to it, and behaving accordingly. Somewhere in life we have learned that we have these powers... but we don't!

The only way to be clear on what one's behavior is about is to ask them. The next time someone does something that confuses you, ask them what is it that they want by doing what they are doing. You may be surprised by the answer!

ANOTHER ONE OF THOSE DAYS

Did you ever have one of those days when nothing seems to go your way? Yesterday seemed that way. When I got up I felt rested. I slept in to 8:00 am. This does not usually happen so already I had a late start to my day. I can easily shrug that off because the day before we drove two and a half hours both ways to a funeral and that definitely was a reason to feel tired.

I tried to write my e-mail mail out but nothing would come, until I told myself to just write. I finally got that done but not without a struggle. I just did not feel like working even though I had jobs to do that I wanted to get done.

Suddenly, my Skype started ringing. I had a coaching session booked, but it was for me to receive some coaching that I had forgotten about. The thing is at the end of previous week I had done what was requested of me and I was ready for the call. So I thought, "Piece of cake here! I have the homework done so all is good."

My coach started out talking about how disheveled she was feeling and apologized for being late! I laughed and said "I would not have known the difference because I forgot completely." We both had a little chuckle. Then I went to get my homework for her and guess what? It had not saved properly on my computer and now nothing was in that file. I thought, "Are the Gods playing tricks on me today or what?" Again we both laughed and continued on.

Remember how I had started the day late? Yes, I ran out of time to get much done. I had a coaching call after lunch and this time I was doing the coaching, but my client came unprepared! She was completely disheveled as I had been earlier in the day. I talked her through some of her frustrations and in the end we made a great plan.

Now I could say I really did not accomplish much yesterday, but that would be untrue. I accomplished lots — just not what I had planned. Tomorrow is another day for those things to get done. I hate it when these types of days happen, but I learned a long time ago that we cannot always have things the way we want them to be. What is more important is how we deal with those off days rather than bemoaning the fact that they happen.

You see, my client spent half of the call speaking negatively to herself and when I asked her how that helps she said it did not! Are we aware of what we are saying to ourselves? Sometimes what we say can be quite harmful. Yes, I am sure we all have days like this and worse. Can you just let go and let be? Tomorrow is a fresh start!

Assumptions

A funny thing happened on our usual Friday night date. We decided to try a new Asian restaurant. The food was good and the atmosphere was upbeat and friendly. It was so friendly that the waitress asked a child sitting in a high chair if he was going to eat all his food for his Mom and Dad!

The man sitting at the table said in a loud voice, "I'm not the FATHER!" A couple of things struck me about his outburst. One was how natural it is that we would assume that this couple was the mother and father of the child. The waitress was a little embarrassed as she apologized.

The other thing that struck me was the manner in which this young man vehemently declared that he wasn't the father of this child. The child's mother hung her head and appeared to be somewhat upset, but then that is my perception. The child did not even notice, but I can't help but wonder how different this scene could have been had the man simply said that he was a friend of the family, an uncle, or someone else.

Dinner was over and it came time to leave. We paid our bill and left the restaurant. As we did another couple was holding the door for us to come out while they were waiting to come in. She looked at us and said," Well, are you all fed up?" That struck me as funny. I know that she meant to say "Are you all filled up?"

Think about it. It was a really funny thing to say especially after my thoughts about the other conversation.

How often do we make assumptions without knowing all the facts? How often do we accidentally say the wrong word? Life can be funny if we pay attention to the little twists and turns.

Awareness

"Awareness: transitioning a reaction to a response." This is a definition I heard just yesterday about awareness. I was listening to someone share their workplace experience they had been through with their employees.

You see, to him his employees are like valuable buildings. As an entrepreneur, he wants to work more *on* his business instead of *in* his business, so he handed the physical tasks of cleaning to his employees. The very first job he gave them to do on their own, he got a complaint from the customer, and he became very upset with is employees and yelled at them. Instead of speaking with his staff about the importance of not getting complaints and doing quality work, he simply overreacted with anger.

He immediately went to the customer's place, did the job himself, and begged for forgiveness from the owner. In hindsight he became aware that he did not like his own behavior on many levels. You see, he reacted too quickly and screamed at his employees. We all know that this will not get him closer to what he wants which is continuous quality in cleaning.

He realized this as well. He suddenly became aware that he did not help himself or his employees. His reaction was a brief involuntary response! But he realized that had he been more consciously aware of what he really wants and more aware of his choices, he could have avoided that eruption.

So what are the alternatives to his behavior? He could have just let it go and said nothing, but this could have led to resentment. He decided to speak to his staff and tell them his own revelation, and how he will do better in the future. He also explained more clearly what his expectations are in terms of always providing quality service. What this man did was transition his reaction to a response which gives him more effective control the next time such a situation arises.

I share this story because it could be any one of us in any situation. Do you pay attention to your behavior and take control of it? It sounds simple, but it is not easy. It is like anything else in life though. Practice helps. The more we become mindful, the better we will feel.

Children And Sex

"Our children have tons of questions about their bodies and sexuality, but how do we talk to them about it?" This is a very common question I get from parents.

I had a wonderful opportunity to meet a very special doctor early on in my journey in teaching sexual health. I was attending a seminar where I met Dr. Mary Calderone, a Public Health doctor from the US. I was excited to meet her and share with her that I had read her book *Talking to Children About Sex*. In front of a room full of people, she screamed at me and challenged me that I had not read her book! I was shocked.

She used me at the time to teach a very strong point! She went on to explain to the group that I had made an error that she wanted to correct right then and there. She stated that the title of her book is *Talking With Children About Sex*. She went on to explain that we never talk "to" children; we talk "with" children. I felt so stupid and embarrassed, but I thanked her after for her poignant message! It was one that I've never forgotten!

You see, whenever we talk *to* people we run the risk of coming off sounding like we are lecturing them. When we talk *with* people, we are engaging in a conversation. It does not matter whether you are conversing with a child or another adult, it is all the same. Once again, it is about the quality of the relationship.

Statistically we know that children want to learn about sex from their parents. They may act like they don't want to talk about it, but they do want to hear about it from you. Here is a tip. Do not talk about *their* sexuality! Use the newspaper, the internet, a story on TV to discuss what is going on with the people in that instance, and ask your children for their opinion of what they have heard or seen.

The same goes with a younger child. When they ask you a question about sex, ask them what they think the answer is and then you can agree or give them the correct answer. Talking about sex with youth, or anyone for that matter, is a process. It is not a deliberate "Let's sit down and talk about sex" mandated conversation. If an opportunity arises from a question they ask, seize the moment to have a discussion around their curiosity.

My son told me recently, "All that stuff you used to say to me, I was listening. And those books you left lying around, I read them all." As parent's we need to equip our youth with the necessary tools for them to enjoy a healthy life and our sexuality is part of that equation.

Control What You Can Control

Recently I was working with someone who said she wanted to be happy like she had been a little over a year ago. I asked her to elaborate on her statement. What did that happiness look like I asked her. She responded "I was full of confidence and my life was in order. I thought I was free and clear of responsibilities with my adult children."

She then said, "Well, one child is getting a divorce and I worry about her. I have someone at work that harasses me, and our teams are not doing as well as they could. On top of everything, I have someone at work who unloads on me all the time."

"What do you mean unloads?" I asked her. "She tells me all her problems, which I don't mind listening to, but then when it comes to work, she tries to control me and tell me what to do" she responded.

I reframed all that she said and then asked her to listen to what she'd just said to me. I then asked her where she had control in her life. She looked at me and replied, "I do not have control in any of those areas. That's the problem!!!"

How often do we permit ourselves to get wrapped up in the issues of others to the detriment of ourselves? Are *you* a fixer? This person wanted to fix everyone else's problems, thinking that she would then be happy. She was taking responsibility for everyone's behavior.

Upon reflection, she realized that she had permitted herself to spiral downward in her own happiness due to things she had no control over. She looked at me and laughed out loud. It is really amazing what you can do to yourself, isn't it? I just grinned at her.

She said that as of that moment, she was going to let all of those people own their problems and she would focus on what she could control. I asked her what that was and she said she was going to make a list of her responsibilities as she announced she already felt better.

Sometimes we need to bring our total behavior into our conscious awareness and self-evaluate about what we can and cannot do. Do you stop and check in with yourself on a regular basis?

Coping With Snow

I had the best time with our snowstorms this past year and Facebook. I love that we are able to learn from and teach others this way! I posted pictures of our car buried in the snow which prompted some friends from overseas to ask questions about how we deal with all this white stuff we get here on the East Coast of Canada. Their question made me stop and think as sometimes we are just so used to something we do not give it a second thought.

These types of happenings are out of our conscious awareness. We just go about doing what we do to move the snow around so we can get our cars out and do what we need to do. Here are the questions I got from some of my Facebook friends:

"Do cars start easily after being under the snow or do they need special attention?" I am so used to a car that always starts I did not think much about this, but sometimes cars do freeze up and refuse to start, but we boost them and start running again.

"Does moisture get inside the car?" It is really too cold for there to be moisture inside from the snow on the outside. The cars are pretty air tight so the answer to that one is no.

"Do you have special antifreezes, components for your car made especially for your weather?" I had not given this much thought either but yes, we do. Our cars are definitely built for this weather.

"How do you get the snow off?" Doug started with our roof rake, then a broom, then a small broom, and finally an ice scraper that we keep in the car.

"How long did it take to clean your car off? Do people go to work after these big storms?" It took Doug about 4 hours to clean the yard after the plow guy did a big chunk of it.

"A snow plow comes down the street and you do the rest of it? Do you climb out a window to get started?" No, I have never experienced anything like this, although I've heard that it's happened to some people.

It was fun to be asked these questions and to answer them so they in turn can pass it on to others. How we deal with the snow in Canada!

Now I was tempted to embellish on the truth a bit, but thought better of it. Really we are so used to it, it (usually) is not that bad. I guess when life hands you snow, you just... make a snowman!

CREATE YOUR OWN PICTURE!

What does your ideal life look like? What really speaks to you? What is absolutely non-negotiable in your life? Your vision is made up of your values and purpose brought together in your quality world! Remember: your quality world is the most important part of your brain in that it is the pictures you have in your head that are most important to you.

Are you living a purpose driven life? Do you have pictures in your quality world of the ideal life for you? Are you coming from a place of survival, success, or significance? Let's look at these three words as they relate to our quality world.

SURVIVAL

To me survival is about getting only what is necessary to get by. I know a young man who is barely doing enough to get by and has no clear vision or purpose for himself. This is a mindset of way to many people in this world.

SUCCESS

This is about achieving most of those pictures you have in your quality world. This is why it is so important to pay attention to what you are placing in your own quality world. If you can't see the success you aspire to get, how will you ever know you have achieved it?

SIGNIFICANCE

This is about legacy and living an intentional life. This is about living with intention to influence and help others move forward with their lives.

Success and significance is what you do with the inevitable challenges and problems that come your way. Your vision, the pictures in your quality world, is what compels you through your most difficult times.

Your vision/quality world needs to incorporate every aspect of what success looks like for you. Take time and think into this.

CREATING A KIOSK

Today, I started calculating the time, energy, and effort it takes me to get a display ready for a kiosk at a conference. For the last four or five months it has been all about creation and design.

Let me back up and look at the total picture. What is needed for a display? It needs to be attractive and professional looking. The first thing I want is a good, high quality banner. The banner takes a few hours to design working with a designer. Then you pay someone to design it and have it created at a sign shop. Thinking into what you want on your banner takes time, let's say a couple of hours. By the time all is said and done that banner is now worth over $500.00. (This includes paying he designer and the sign shop.)

Then there are the marketing materials. Brochures are a big part of that mix. I market Reality Therapy, Choice Theory Training, so I wanted new brochures this year. The content was simple and it does not often change, but the appearance and structure takes time to work on. Another few hours pass by.

Then we wanted something to hand out to participants at the workshop. This year it was new habits cards. I presented last year and could use the same ones, but they did not match my new banner, etc. I wanted something new so a bookmark was created. Not only were the habits cards and bookmarks recreated, they were done bilingually with the same process as the brochures and the banner. This all takes time for me and my team, plus the materials have to be sent to the printers to the tune of a little over $400.00 just for printing! We can add to that the cost to do the display of over $300.00.

So why am I telling you all of this? I am not saying this to brag. In fact, I really cannot afford to do all this, but I cannot afford not to either. If I want to attract top clients then I need to look good and professional. It is like the chicken or the egg, which comes first. I have learned after many years of working from a shoestring budget that I just have to go for it. I am sure I will reap the benefits as time goes on.

You see, coaching, speaking, and training are intangible items. It is difficult for the average person to recognize the value added that most coaches bring to the table. When we can cost out the value, something as simple as preparing for a conference for which you are paying to attend, it shows some tangible evidence of the value. This does not include the years and years of personal growth and development that the presenter has put in to learn the information they will share with their audience.

What do you do to add value? Do you see the tangibles? The intangibles? Do you recognize your value and worth? I am looking forward to sharing my new handouts, etc. upcoming conferences. Meeting all the people will be the main fun. Adding value to others is my goal.

CURIOSITY SAVED THE CAT

What's the single most valuable asset for personal success? Drive, commitment, passion, risk-taking?

All of the above play a part, of course, but there's something fundamental to our success that very few people give much thought to. It's a single word describing a single behavior.

CURIOSITY!

Curiosity is the fuel that drives us to step into the unknown and to become more than we are today. Curiosity is what compels us to get out of the rut that is our comfort zone.

Unfortunately, being curious has a stigma attached to it. There are deep-seated connotations for being curious.

When we're young we're told through various methods that curiosity is dangerous. It's life-threatening to a cat. "Curiosity killed the cat" we're told. It got Curious George into endless trouble. In "grown up" land being curious is often viewed as silly or immature, and to be curious in a conversation can be considered intrusive.

These are very limiting perspectives because curiosity is what brings you and I the ideas that grow and improve our lives. Sadly, for reasons already outlined, developing curiosity isn't a priority for most people, and that's a **big mistake.**

Curiosity fuels questions, and questions fuel growth by drawing out the answers that take us forward.

Einstein said "The important thing is to not stop questioning. Curiosity has its own reason for existing." Brian Tracy, a successful entrepreneur, said "A major stimulant to creative thinking is focused questions. There is something about a well-worded question that often penetrates to the heart of the matter and triggers ideas and insights."

CUSTOMER SERVICE

Today I was interviewed by Craig Pollack, a podcaster. Craig is a main street business coach from Baltimore. He found me on LinkedIn and thought I would make a great guest for his show. His is a coach for small main street businesses. He invited me to talk about customer service. When he asked me to do this, I was hesitant because my immediate thought was, "I don't know anything about customer service!"

But wait a minute. I am an owner of a small business. I know what it is like to be a customer, and how I like to be served! He obviously read something on my LinkedIn profile that led him to believe I was somewhat of an expert on this subject.

What I am is an expert in Human Behavior! Today we talked about what great customer service is and just exactly who is our customer. I suggested that our number one customer is our employees and it is important to have an understanding of human behavior to provide strong leadership.

We talked about the five needs that we are motivated to satisfy, but more importantly, we talked about the pictures we carry in our head about how we satisfy those needs. We talked about creating a trusting relationship with our employees and how important it is to help our employees meet these needs in the workplace. If your employees are happy, then guess what – your customers will be happy.

We also discussed being an entrepreneur, working long hours, and feeling trapped in a business. We talked about the importance of being able to trust and delegate tasks to others so that we can live a healthy lifestyle.

Not too many people enter the entrepreneurial life to work 16-18 hour days. They usually enter it to have freedom, yet, they get locked into their "baby" so to speak, and have difficulty letting go. Do you have difficulty letting go of delegation? What are you hanging on to that you know you would be better off and even healthier, physically, mentally, emotionally and spiritually without having?

You see, we all need to think about these things and take responsibility for our own health and happiness. Are you aware of this and what are you doing about it?

Dealing With Conflict

One day as I was working quietly in my office at the sexual health center, I heard a rather frantic knock on my door. The center was closed that morning and I was catching up on paperwork. At first I ignored the knocking, but then it became louder and more frantic. I could not let this continue and decided to open the door. What if it was a young teenager in trouble, looking for help?

As I opened the door, a rather harried, frantic mother, almost pushed me out of the way, saying "I need to talk to a nurse here! I was told to come see you!" I explained who I was and what services we offered. She then told me that she wanted to know if her daughter was pregnant. I then asked her how old her daughter was.

She said that she was sixteen years old. Hearing this, I simply said, "I am sorry, but I cannot give you any information about your daughter. I cannot even tell you if your daughter has even visited the clinic. You see, she is sixteen years old and under the law I cannot give out any information about her."

This woman became enraged and started screaming at me! She told me that I was like all the other people she had talked with in her quest for information. She said (in a very loud voice): "You in your fancy office and your fancy clothes! You are just like the rest of them!" "Who have you already seen?", I asked. "I went to the police station, the Social Works Department, and even saw a lawyer. They all refused to tell me anything and I am damned mad!" She slammed her hand down on my desk and continued, saying "IF YOU DON'T TELL ME WHAT I WANT TO KNOW, YOU WILL SOON BE DEAD!"

I was frightened and immediately called my supervisor who simply told me that she was in a meeting and I would have to call security or handle it myself. I called for security, but they did not answer. What was I going to do?

It had not been that long since I started my Reality Therapy training so I drew on my inner resources and remembered what I had learned there. I looked at her and said, "I can see you are very upset and I sincerely wish I could help you. Do you think you could have a seat and we could chat?"

Just acknowledging and accepting her feelings, she immediately felt as if someone was listening to her. I told her that I still couldn't give her any information, but what I could do was help her figure out a way to find out the information she desperately wanted to know from her daughter. She told me that her daughter had told her she was pregnant, and the mother really believed that her daughter should not have a baby. She felt it best that if she was pregnant, she was going to make her have an abortion!

We continued to chat. We talked about her relationship with her daughter to which she agreed they did not get along at all. We talked about using external control and how that affected their relationship. She went away with a plan to use only caring habits with her daughter and promised to let me know how it worked out.

She called me about a week later and brought her daughter to see me. They were getting along better. In fact, her daughter was not pregnant nor had she ever had sex. She and her boyfriend had broken up. Her mother brought her to see the clinic so she would know where she could go if ever she needed birth control.

All this mother wanted was someone to listen to her and give her some tools to deal with a situation she was terrified of mishandling. One of the best ways to deal with conflict is to acknowledge the feelings and then use the procedures that lead to change.

Depression Cutting into Productivity

"Study finds unrecognized depression cutting into productivity." This was the headline in my local newspaper recently. Canadians and their co-workers might be depressed and not realize they need help according to a report on workplace health.

The lead author of the study was Dr. Carolyn Dewa of the Center for Addiction and Mental Health, which is affiliated with the University of Toronto. I am not going to report the whole article here, but here's the bottom line. The article stated: "It's important for employers to know where to start when it comes to tackling productivity loss related to untreated depression," Dewa said in the news release.

Do we send employees who are depressed off for mental health treatment and potentially drugs, or do we look into the culture of the workplace? The article said 40% of respondents were experiencing significant symptoms of depression, but more than half of that group (52.8 %) did not recognize the need to seek help.

Can that many people really be unhappy in the workplace? With my experience as someone who worked with Employee Assistance Programs, there was nearly always a relationship somewhere that was not the way they wanted it to be. Do we really respect each other in the workplace? Are we recognized for the work we do? These are just a few of the many additional questions that need to be asked. What role does bullying or external control play in the workplace?

Making broad statements like this concerns me. The article went on to say that the employees should be seeking help. I do not have a problem with that, but what are we doing to create quality work places in the first place?

Obviously these people are unable to meet their duties in their workplace or they are in a job they do not want to be in. There are so many factors to uncovering the cause of depression, but what does this article say about our world or work environment if so many are suffering?

Do I Need This Challenge?

I competed in the Division E Toastmasters International Speech Contest in 2015. This means that I made it through the competition at the club level, then the area speech contests, and then went on to participate in the Division section. To compete at this level, or any other for that matter, it takes a lot of hard work.

First, you have to craft your speech and it must be your original work. Then you work at it, fine tune it, and keep adding, changing, practicing, etc. until the words roll off your tongue. For example, for the past two weeks, I had my speech where I wanted it to be, and I practiced it no less than five to six times daily!

I am ready to head to the contest. I chose to do this and I added this stress to my life. Now I am asking myself, "Are you completely crazy? Why do you do this to yourself?" There are many answers to these questions. Yes, I am crazy, but then I have always enjoyed an opportunity to stretch my limits. But really, does it have to be this way?

I spoke, gave a great speech, received excellent feedback, but I did not win the contest. You see, for me it was not about winning the contest. It was about seizing the opportunity to stretch myself yet again and compete in a contest where other contestants had actually been on the international stage at least four times. I had actually been coached by one of them! What was I thinking? Compete against my coach? Of course, Maureen, now that makes sense!

Seriously though, it does make sense. It gave me an opportunity to try out new ideas, new methods of presentation, and I added value to the audience at the same time. Never underestimate an opportunity like this!

As I pondered it a little longer, it did distract me from some other work that I had on my plate. As a result, I am behind in some of the things I wanted to accomplish. I have to ask myself, is this really what I want to be doing with my time?

I am going to focus on this for a while because as a speaker, one thing I know is "Speakers Speak", but do I really need to put myself through this? It was fun and now I will be supporting the winner as he readies himself for the next level.

As for me, I will be preparing myself for a TED Talk the end of June! I just love a challenge.

Dreams! No Goals! No Life!

Let's talk about goals and growth. Do you have a quality world picture of your ideal life in the coming year? What about 2020 or 2025? You see, I believe we all have pictures in our heads of desires to move ourselves forward. We have aspirations to be more, have more, and feel more fulfilled. We dream about those things on a regular basis.

This is what is speaking to you at your core. Are you listening? I have learned that if you do not take time out and listen to yourself and focus on what your dreams and aspirations are, no one else will do it for you. Are you going to be intentional from this day forward?

Do you allow yourself to be still and focus on what your best life would be like if you could be living it today? You see, I believe we are all born with talents and values, and that it is our job to use our talents to help others move forward. We need to value ourselves enough to do what we love and chose work that utilizes our strengths and talents.

I can hear some of you saying, "Yes, I have my dreams, but..." and here come the excuses! We can create as many roadblocks to our dreams as we want, or we can assess our dreams and actually start to work towards them. We do this by setting some goals and actions that will move us in that direction.

Sadly, some people will sell themselves a bill of goods that goes something like this: "Sure I have my dreams, but they will never happen!" If you believe this statement then you've already set yourself up for failure.

Others will say, "Yes, I have dreams, and I know someday they will work out." Others still will say, "Yes, I have my dreams, and I am going to do everything I can to have them come to fruition starting today! It may take some time, but I know I will work with intention and they will come true!"

Which person are you? Do you have a growth plan to get yourself to where you want to be? We cannot get to our destination without a map. You would not drive to a new destination without learning what you need to know to get there and without a GPS or a map.

EVERYTHING BEGINS IN THOUGHT

Everything begins in thought. When you take on the thoughts of a winner, you'll know how to win. That's an interesting statement, isn't it?! Could it be that simple? Think like a winner and become a winner? I think it is a whole lot better option than the opposite.

What is the opposite of that? If you think you are a loser, guess what you are? It is impossible to win if you see yourself as a loser.

Everything begins in thought. What this means is that everything is created twice. Dr. Glasser would explain this by discussing what happens in the creative system of our brain. The brain is an amazing organ. It is continually organizing and reorganizing behaviors.

When we come to a situation we are not familiar with, the brain will search for behaviors that we already have that may work for us or it will create a new behavior. Dr. Glasser taught us that once a behavior is created it becomes an organized behavior. This was why he said that those that go on shooting rampages had to have the thought first and therefore it is an organized behavior over which they have control. They carried out the shootings after they created the idea.

Entrepreneurs have an idea before they begin their business. We know the effect negative thinking can have on our health. It creates more stress and more stress affects the cells of our body. So when you take on the thoughts of a winner, it is easy to understand you will know how to win.

Are there winners in your life? What are their thoughts like? Do you watch what they do? Do you ever ask them how they do what they do or what they are thinking?

Just some food for thought. What do you think winners do? And better yet, are you doing the same things yourself?

Excuse Me, Please!

Lately, I caught myself coming up with plausible excuses why I was late in mailing out my weekly article. We all know that excuses are all about external control and that simply by offering excuses I am saying that something or someone outside of me is controlling what I do.

That is not true.

However, I am going to give you my excuses anyway simply to show I am human and that it is in our nature to offer excuses for our behavior. Here are my top three:

1. *I was Chairperson at our Toastmaster's meeting the night before and I was too busy getting ready for that so did not have time to write the article.*
2. *The Blue Jays were playing the Kansas City Royals on TV and I could not miss the game.*
3. *The Federal Election results were on all evening and late into the night, so I was busy watching television.*

It would seem these are reasonable excuses, but sadly, they are not. You see, I could have made the letter a bigger priority and had it written over the weekend, but I am glad I did not do that because now I have something of value to share with you about excuses. See? There is always a different choice.

Last night I went to bed late knowing that I had a breakfast meeting this morning and I gave myself permission to miss it. I did not miss the meeting though because I woke up at 6:30 am and couldn't sleep any longer so decided to get up and go.

The interesting thing is that other people were late for the breakfast meeting and every single one of them used two out of the three excuses I shared with you above. Yes, you guessed it, numbers 2 and 3. The sad thing is most of the people that were at this meeting truly believe that it is the fault of the Blue Jays and Justin Trudeau that they were late! How bizarre is that?

You see, every one of us could have made a different choice, but it was satisfying to stay up late and watch the Jays win and see what our political future will look like. Would it have been more appropriate to say something like "I chose to be late this morning because I stayed up to see the outcome of the Jays game and the election?" Yes, it would be, and, in fact, when people said that, I responded with "I chose to stay up late too, knowing full well I could be tired and late this morning." I got some laughs, but mostly people did not realize I was talking about making that a conscious choice!

We are so engrained in the external world that many lack conscious awareness of the choices we make and give excuses that nine times out of ten are accepted as status quo. Beware of your excuses as sometimes you may very well get caught in a lie.

EXPANDED BELIEFS

Over the period of one weekend we held a basic practicum in Choice Theory, Reality Therapy and Lead Management with lots of learning through role-play and discussion. Role-playing is one of the most valuable tools of this training. I want to emphasize the play portion because although the clients we work with are familiar to us, we are not in their heads. For the most part, the roles are made up, but doing role-play is an opportunity to try an approach and see how it works out.

I am always excited when I see people's eyes light up either because it worked very well or because they become aware of something they may or may not be doing in their day-to-day living. Having a group of warm, supportive people around us adds to the opportunity for growth.

Sometimes, though, we have some limiting beliefs. Right now some of you are reading this and saying to yourselves, "Really? Role play? I hate role play." I am willing to bet that this is due to a belief that you learned somewhere in your past, either in school or some other setting, and you've adopted this belief as fact. It has now become a firmly entrenched limiting belief in your mind.

In the middle of the night I awoke thinking about this whole concept of limiting beliefs and how we have our beliefs in our quality worlds and how Dr. Glasser talked about being careful of what we put in our quality world. Our quality world is a small space in our brain where we store pictures of people, places, things and strong beliefs that are satisfying to us. How many limiting beliefs do you have built up in your quality world? Are you willing to examine them?

In order to change a quality world picture, we need another picture to add to our quality world that is equally need satisfying. What if I were to suggest that we focus on "expanding beliefs" instead? You see, the more we expand our beliefs, the more open we become, the less judgmental we will be, and the happier our lives will be as well.

Five Mice and Me

A couple of weeks ago I had a crazy dream that has kept me pondering until now. You might say it has been gnawing away at me. (Pun intended and you'll soon learn why!) Let me tell you the story.

In my dream, I awake from my sleep to find a little grey mouse holding tightly to my right ear, refusing to let go of it. Every time I take it off my ear it opens its mouth with big, ugly teeth, snarls at me, and continues to grab my right ear.

In the meantime, there are four other mice running out of my bedroom closet scattering every which way. At no time did I feel frightened. In fact, they were a very clean, light grey, bunch of creatures. But there was one gnawing away at me although he did not chew though my ear. He was just hanging on to me for dear life.

I have thought about this dream over and over. Then this week I downloaded the audio version of the book *Think and Grow Rich.* In the book, Napoleon Hill talks about purpose: being of definite purpose and of the importance of desire, persistence, and faith. Suddenly I had these thoughts.

The mouse on my ear represents persistence. The ones running around are without direction and are seemingly going nowhere. When I truly desire something, then I need to be as tenacious as that mouse on my ear, and have faith that the persistence will pay off in volumes when it comes to getting what I truly desire.

I am reminded of my friend Joe who is competing annually to become the world champion of speakers at Toastmasters International. He has the desire to win. He consistently and persistently focuses on his dream. Twice now in the last five years he has made it to the top 8 in the world. As long as he continues to have that desire, remains persistent in trying, and has the faith that he can do it, I am sure he will make it!

There is no such thing as getting something for nothing. What do you desire? Are you focused and persistently going after it? Do you truly believe it is possible?

Full Moon or What?

There are days when we go about our business and things go very well. Then there are days when it seems like everyone is being an idiot. Do you ever have those kinds of days?

Recently we went out to do our usual Saturday routine. We go out for breakfast as a treat and this day before we'd travelled too far down the road to the restaurant, we were cut off in traffic twice, and saw a car cross over two lanes of traffic to make a wrong way turn!

I looked at Doug and said it must be a full moon or something. We chuckled and carried on. This all happened within two kilometers of home and within the timespan of ten minutes. There are days like that, but is it really full moon causing it or are people just going about their way unconsciously?

After our breakfast, we carried on with our day. We went back home because I had received one of those letters from the car dealership with an offer you cannot refuse and we wanted to go check this out. They were going to give me a newer car and reduce my payments at the same time. We picked up the letter and headed across town. For a Saturday morning at 10:30 am, the streets were almost empty! Wow, such an easy drive. So we made our trip to the market, dropped into the mall for a few minutes, and headed on to the car dealership.

As we are driving along in the left-hand lane, a black car in front of us decided to slow down. As he did he put his hand out the window and gave us the middle finger, so Doug just pulled into the right hand lane because we were going to turn up that road anyway. Just as we did that, the black car decided he wanted to pull into the same lane, almost like he was threatening us! The driver and the co-passenger were making all kinds of gestures until we got beside them, when they suddenly stopped! Weird!

We figured they were after someone who drives the same vehicle as us and when they saw who was driving our car, they backed off. Go figure! Now, we know that all behavior is purposeful, but really, what was this all about? For a few minutes it was a dangerous situation. We wondered what the purpose of that behavior was all about. He certainly was aware of what he was doing.

As, I sit here writing this, I am thankful that we arrived home safely and were able to enjoy the nice weather for the rest of that day.

Do you come across similar situations? We have a choice how to act when they happen to us. We chose to ignore the irate driver. What would you have done in that situation?

GET RID OF SUPER WOMAN!

Every now and then I just feel like pulling my hair out. I know that I come from the generation of Super Women. You see, I am in the first "so called" generation of women to have worked full-time outside the home. With that decision came many challenges. We still had all the work to do at home as well as the full-time job elsewhere.

Many of today's women persist in trying to copy their mothers and grandmothers behavior by believing they can do it all. You see, we said you can do anything you want, but what today's woman heard was you can do it all!

In the early years of my marriage and while looking after a small child, I did work outside the house full-time. I did so without the benefit of a dishwasher and washer and dryer, initially, but eventually we had to buy those items so we could survive. Many of us did all the housework as well, hating it the whole time. The men continued to do so called "man chores" outside of their full-time work.

Why am I on this rant today? I met a young woman at a networking event and she was intrigued that I am a coach. She asked me if I coach consultants. We had a short conversation and she told me her biggest challenge is time management. You see, she has two preschool aged children and one in early elementary school. She was wishing for more time to see clients and be able to spend more time with her children. I asked her if she had a bookkeeper to which she responded, "Oh no, not yet. You see I can do it myself pretty easily." I wondered how long it takes her to do that part of her business.

Then I asked her who does the housework and she told me that she does it all. She has a more traditional marital relationship and her husband does all the outside chores while she takes care of the inside ones. I asked her how long it takes to do the simple cleaning herself and what she could do with that time if someone else were to do it for her. I then asked her if she enjoyed doing it to which she responded that she hated it. But again, she repeated that it was too expensive to hire someone else to do it.

I wanted to jump out of my chair and shake her. Don't worry. I maintained my cool. You see it comes down to beliefs, values, and priorities. If her children are her priority and she wants more time with them, then something has to go. She believes that only rich people hire housekeepers. I asked her if she thought about the fact she would be contributing to the economy by hiring someone to do the work she does not like to do. She had not thought of this solution in that manner.

I am of the belief that just because we can do something, it does not mean we should do it. Why is it that we need to fall into the Super Woman trap? Think about it. For a mere fifty dollars or so a week or every other week for someone to clear her house would give her at least a half-day to do fun things with her children, or de-clutter a closet, or even see a new client.

As I was discussing this in my inner circle, one of the businessmen said this: "I agree 100% with you, Maureen. I hire a housekeeper, gardener, and a home handyman and that's just for my personal life. I refuse to wash my own cars, etc. Like you, I am capable of doing all of it myself, but my time has value."

Remember: we do not have to do it all just because we can! Let someone else be Super Woman!

Gig Cancelled!

Sometimes things are just plain funny! Today, as I was planning my week, I received a message that a speaking engagement that was coming up had been cancelled! Pay attention to what happened next and the language that I used when telling my partner about it!

I looked at Doug and said, "Well, I guess you can have me for dinner after all!" He looked at me and said, "But I don't want you for dinner!"

I responded, "What? Really!" I was thinking he would rather cook what he wanted for supper, perhaps something that I don't like rather than have me eat dinner with him! He could see I was not impressed and he replied, "I don't want to eat you for supper! I think a pork chop would be much better!"

This was him being particular about my choice of language. Then I told him that I thought he would rather eat shrimp or something than have dinner with me. He laughed out loud as did I. We could see how silly the whole conversation had been between us.

Can you see how easily we can go down a slippery slope just with our choice of words? It really was funny!

Today is craft day with my friends so instead of travelling to my speaking gig, I will be visiting with them. And when I come home we will dine together and enjoy our evening before I take off for my annual business retreat tomorrow.

Think about your language and the words you use! Where are your funny stories?

GRAMMY MO'S STICKY SITUATION

Today I spent a little time questioning why my keyboard was so sticky. I kept telling myself that I must wipe it off. It also crossed my mind that more than once during the past two or three days my fingers were getting stuck on my mouse pad!

Do you ever put up with something for far too long? This is what I did in this case. Without being aware, I was grumbling to myself about the sticky keys and every time my fingers did not slide smoothly across them, I felt a little irritated.

Today, suddenly I realized that my computer was sticky because my grandchildren had been visiting over the weekend. You see, I had allowed them to watch a video on my computer!

At the same time, this wonderful grandmother gave them oranges and bananas to eat while watching their video. Because it was my grandchildren, in true grandmotherly fashion, I accepted responsibility for giving them not only access to my computer, but also the fruit! With that knowledge, I enjoyed a silent smile and immediately went and got the cloth needed to wipe down my computer keyboard.

Now my hand is sliding easily across the keys. I began to think about this escapade and how wonderful it is to be a grandparent and not get bent out of shape over something a child had done quite innocently. This is a behavior very different than the behavior might of been had it been my son doing the same thing at that same age! No, I am not going there on the guilt train!

How wonderful it would have been to have the wisdom then that I have now. But then if I did, there would be no need for Grammy Mo! Do you ever find yourself in sticky situations? How do you handle them? Do you focus on the relationship and search for the solution, or do you blame someone for the problem that was created?

Relationships are key and it is really important that we focus on what is most important in the situation. Remember to ask yourself, "Is what I am going to do or say bring me closer or further apart from this person I want and need in my life?"

GUARD WELL YOUR SPARE MOMENTS

"Guard well your spare moments. They are like uncut diamonds. Discard them and their value will never be known. Improve them and they will become the brightest gems in a useful life."

— Ralph Waldo Emerson

Today I am taking a bit of a break. I gave myself permission to take some time this morning just to reflect on my week. I was thinking about this quote about guarding well your spare moments. I think it is important that we find those spare moments to think and reflect on how we are doing daily. If not, our life will be like those uncut diamonds. We will lose those moments and never get them back.

We will flow through life taking what comes and will wonder why we cannot get more of what we want. Today we are all busy doing something, especially if we are hooked on social media. I make it a practice to reflect for at least a half hour every morning. I review my day in the evening and I plan the next day before I go to bed. I have a much better chance of succeeding at achieving my goals by practicing this method.

I had a good friend who worked with me for six months when I was teaching sexual health. I had a teenage son at the time and we were on the go regularly with his basketball team. I was overwhelmed with so much to do and had so little time that I would forget to do some things and get frustrated.

My friend, who was a little older than me and quite wise, sat me down one day and said, "Maureen, may I make a suggestion to you?" I said "Sure, go ahead." She then said, "You seemed to miss a lot of things and I simply wanted to suggest that you make a daily list of the things you want to get done. It might help you better organize your day."

I now go one step further and do more than she suggested. I prioritize my "to do" list and carry what I don't get done over to the next day. As simple as this sounds it was (and still is) very sound advice. I have been a list maker ever since. It is even more important now that I have my own business.

Are you a list maker? What would happen if you wrote the top six things you needed to get done every day? What difference do you think that would make?

Maybe you already know!

GUILT

I love my life! This week I had conversations with others about guilt on more than one occasion. It has been a long time since I have talked about this topic. I can remember many times in my past when I had been guilt ridden. In fact, there was so much guilt it was like I was caught in a trap! How about you? Have you found yourself caught up in the guilt trap recently?

So what is guilt?

> *"Guilt is a cognitive or an emotional experience that occurs when a person realizes or believes—accurately or not—that he or she has compromised his or her own standards of conduct or has violated a moral standard, and bears significant responsibility for that violation. It is closely related to the concept of remorse."*
>
> – Jerry Jampolsky, MD.

Note that guilt is a cognitive or emotional experience. That means that thinking is a big part of it and where do we have the most control in our total behavior? In our thinking and acting. You see, I had a ton of limiting beliefs that I inherited from adults in my younger life, and imposing guilt was a behavior used in an attempt to control me.

Guilt is one of those emotions that we can easily use to express that we are feeling sorry for a behavior we chose without actually having to say we're sorry.

> *"Very simply, guilt can be defined as the feeling of self-condemnation that we experience after we do something we think is wrong."*
>
> – Jerry Jampolsky, MD.

What purpose does it serve for us to self-condemn? Does this derail our self-esteem, self-worth and confidence? Most definitely.

Here is something to ponder. If you have done something that goes against what you value, you have violated one of your own quality world pictures, and you are responsible for that. But what if you have done something that violates another's value or belief? There are some things to think about. Do you agree with that belief? Is it your belief or does it belong to someone else?

If you are choosing guilt, it may be that you are trying to force yourself to do something you don't want to do and you are doing it mainly to please someone else. This is external control again as you attempt to please someone else.

Think about it. If you feel remorse for a behavior you have chosen, why not admit you were in the wrong? Give yourself the gift of forgiveness and move on. It sounds simple, but remember the alternative is to remain stuck where you are at which isn't healthy.

Guilt is a wasted emotion designed to keep us stuck. We do have a choice whether to stay there or move on!

GOALS WITHOUT VISION

"Goals are a natural consequence of a growth-oriented person's life." I love this quote from my coach, Christian Simpson. If you are on a personal growth journey right now, stop and think about the goals you have automatically created for yourself. Goals are great, but if you do not know where you are going they mean nothing. I think this may be a reason that people do not take the time to write out their goals.

There is something way more important than goals and that is what it means to live on purpose and come to a vision. We see a lot written about having a vision. If you are in a workplace, you may see your company's vision statement on the wall as you walk the corridors. Are you aware of it? Pay attention. Is it there?

If you do not see or revisit the vision statement with your employer, then how do you know where you are going with your work? Let me put it this way. When you get in your car, you have a clear picture of where you want to go and hopefully a map for getting there. You would not leave home without a vision of where you are going yet we often tackle our work lives without a clear direction of where we are going.

A vision statement is key for personal and professional success, yet the great majority of the population does not have one for themselves. I think in the last few years this practice is becoming more popular with the use of Vision Boards. This tool helps people create images, but the danger here is this can be too vague and now we are walking around in generalities.

What does it mean to really dig deep and find your own personal vision, your picture of where you want to be in one week, one month, one year, five years and so on? If you do not know where you are going how will you get there?

Do you have a very clear, precise image of what a successful life looks like for you? Do you have a picture that encompasses a life living your primary values through your purpose? As my coach says, "Your vision is your values and purpose brought to life on the screen of your mind."

HEADLINE POWER

Recently, I picked up the newspaper and the headline read:

> *"Nearly half of women find senior roles unattractive, study says."*

I could not believe what I was reading. It certainly got my attention. You see, my perception was that the article was going to talk about women not liking themselves as they got older, and I was thinking surely this is not so, since the older I get, the less that matters to me.

I checked with Doug to see what his perception was based on the headline and he laughed and said that he questioned the headline too. I am not sure if it was a grammatical error on purpose or a great ploy to get women and men alike to read the article.

What would your perception be of a headline like this?

I had to read the article to check my perception to see if I was correct.

The article, in fact, had nothing to do whatsoever with women and aging. It was a study that had been conducted to determine why more women do not apply for top executive jobs.

My perception was dead wrong! How often do you read a headline and carry on as if you have all the news of the day? Do you check your perceptions and read further? What does that have to do with communication, I wonder?

By the way, I rarely read the newspaper, but this headline caught my eye. Very clever or not very clever, I am not sure, but I did influence me to read the article!

Healthy People/Healthy Relationships

It takes relationally healthy people to build great relationships. Let's take a look at the essential components suggested by John Maxwell*. I am sharing my thoughts on those components.

The Lens Principle
Who we are determines how we see other people. Consider that immediately from birth we are taking in information from our environment. We can only see people from that environmental lens. There is an expression that says in order to see something in another person we have had to experience it ourselves. This falls in the area of our perceptual system. How we take in information through our five senses and attach a value to it is uniquely our own doing. We do that based on our experiences and the pictures we have in our head, hence the lens!

The Mirror Principle
The first person we must examine is ourselves. This process is called self-evaluation. When we are in a relationship, it is always wise to ask what is our individual role in whatever is going on. Taking a good look at ourselves ensures we know what we're creating.

The Pain Principle
Hurting people hurt people and are easily hurt by them. German poet Herman Hesse wrote, "If you hate a person, you hate something in him that is part of yourself." John Maxwell says when hurting people lash out, it is in response to what is happening in them more than what's happening around them. People who do not believe in themselves will never succeed. This is a huge problem in domestic violence or any other violent situation. It is about the pain that is carried inside. Again, we need to take a good look at ourselves. Unfortunately in this situation, there is a lot of use of the deadly habits.

THE HAMMER PRINCIPLE

As the old saying goes, never use a hammer to swat a fly. To me this says pick your battles wisely. There are so many little things that happen throughout our day that to spend negative energy on the small things as if they were the end of the world just does not cut it.

THE ELEVATOR PRINCIPLE

We can lift people up or take them down. We really cannot control another person. All we can do is attempt to influence them. Do we want to influence them positively or negatively? What is in the best interest of the relationship?

Bottom line? We can choose how we want our relationships to be by monitoring our own behavior.

*Adapted from the writings of John Maxwell

HONORED TO BE IN THE ROOM

As I sat in my writing course the day before Remembrance Day, I was reminded how grateful I was to be there. A gentleman shared his story of war times with us and while unfortunately I am not able to tell you his story, I was filled with gratitude that I was "free" to be in the room due to his fighting for our freedom.

I was also grateful that he would write and share that story. In a very few years his story will be gone and any lessons we could have learned from him will be gone as well. His stories added a depth to war times that we have only heard about, but when someone shares their experience of it, it brings it to reality.

It is such a joy to be in a room with people from ages 55 to 91 as they write and share their stories. There is such richness to their words. It is interesting how nearly everyone who came to the writing course stated they just wanted to write for themselves, yet as the stories unfolded we wanted them to write for us.

As you are reading this, what stories do you have to share? What limiting beliefs keep you from sharing them? Even if you write solely for yourself, do you know the benefits of that aspect alone? Our teacher encouraged us to write by hand, not on the computer, as there is a connection that takes place between the brain and the hand that brings out the emotion and richness of the story.

Do you have stories that could serve others? What about your family? What would you like them to know? Have you written those stories down? Is it time to start?

My story is going to be about a little girl who lost a brother who was eight years old to leukemia when she was ten, and the challenges she faced when the adoption of a new baby brother happened in her family. Does that peak your interest? This is my story and I never really saw it as helping anyone else, but there is a part of me that knows it will.

If you have been thinking about writing, just do it! You will be surprised by what you learn about yourself.

I CAN'T

As I was trying to write today it occurred to me that sometimes it seems there is nothing to write about, but if you just sit quietly it will come to you. You see, we all have all we need inside of us. Many times the reason we cannot accomplish something, like writing a story or book, is because of the stories we tell ourselves.

We say things like "I would love to write a book someday, but I am not a writer." Or "I love how you write, but I could not do that because I do not know what to say. I am just not a writer." We say these things, but we write every day. We write grocery lists, we write school lists for our kids, or we make a note of somewhere we need to be. Some of us even write speeches for a talk we have to give in our workplace, but we tell ourselves we cannot write. I am suggesting that if you just sit quietly for at least fifteen minutes a day and just write, wondrous things will happen. It does not matter if the story makes sense right now. Just let the words flow from your heart.

A few years ago, I decided I wanted to write a book for parents, counselors, and teachers – anyone working with youth concerned about their sexual health. I had no idea where to begin, but I did know that I needed to just start. I sat at my computer every single day for a year until I had finally finished writing that book.

I had a lot of beliefs floating around in my head about what I could and could not do, but I decided I really wanted to do it. It took a while but eventually it all came together. Last year I decided to update that book *Choosing a Quality Loving Sexual Relationship* and soon I am hoping to offer it as an e-book.

I have to tell you that first thing this morning, I thought to myself "What am I going to write today?" I didn't have anything in particular on my mind, but allowing myself to be quiet brought what I was saying to myself into my conscious awareness. You are receiving the results of this morning's quiet time.

What have you been thinking about doing, but telling yourself you can't do? Perhaps it's time to be still, think about it, and come up with a solution.

In today's world we are too easily distracted with all the bells and whistles of things happening around us. Take some time this week for you to sit, be still, and think about what you really want. ***

I Love Wednesdays!

I love Wednesdays!

As some of you know I retired from being in the Public Health sector in 2004, about the same time as many other nurses I know well did. My dream was to retire early and continue as an entrepreneur with my own company, following my dreams and aspirations. There was a promise I made to myself though, whereby I would always reserve time for my family and friends.

This is why I love Wednesdays. I start my day off with a networking meeting at 7:00 am at a local restaurant. We are there to offer leads to each other and to promote our own business and work. We have a speaker and plan our future meetings. When you live most of your life working in government run entities, I now have huge respect for the entrepreneur. Here in New Brunswick, we would not survive if it were not for small business owners!

After I return to my office, I do some writing, catch up on some emails, make a few phone calls, and then I am off to visit my friends. We call it Craft Day. How many crafts actually get started or completed depends on how much talking we do, what party we are planning, what travel is coming up, and how many world problems we are solving.

Sometimes we are simply supporting others in the group through tough times. Sometimes we are laughing about the funny things we have done, and sometimes we are actually doing crafts. One thing is for sure. Dessert and coffee are always served at 3:00 pm.

I love my girlfriends because it's them who ground me. In other words, when I am with them, I am thinking about nothing else but our interactions. It is completely different from my day-to-day work in my business and provides me with a great break to the routine. What do you do to ground yourself or get that much needed break?

Once again life really does revolve around our significant relationships. Where are your significant relationships? What are you doing to nourish them?

I WAS A FOOL

I have made a fool of myself more than once. In Toastmaster's we have an opportunity to practice speaking before an audience that is in your corner. They are there to support and offer you effective feedback. They use a term they call the "sandwich approach," where the speech evaluator offers you what they like about your speech and areas of improvement, and then what they like again. Sound familiar? Of course not, because most of the world wants to criticize us.

When we are getting ready for speech contests, the evaluator's will help us by giving great feedback and assist us in refining our speech. My very first time as a seasoned speaker, I entered the speech contest and won in my club. I was feeling really proud and thought, "This is a piece of cake." I had been speaking most of my adult career and I was good! Well, maybe just a tad arrogant as well!

When I went to the area championships, I got a rude awakening as I did not perform anywhere near the level of the other people who competed. You see, they had been preparing for quite some time and were really good. "Wow," I thought. "This Toastmasters group rocks!" Yes, I lost that competition, but that did not stop me from entering another one down the road.

I compete in the humorous speech contest that happens every fall, but this time I chose to work with a speaker coach, a member of our club. I made it all the way to the District Final's. Now the speech I had prepared was a good one about technology and the imaginary relationships between a small Acer computer and a Blackberry phone. It really was quite funny and it did have some sexual innuendos.

I was fine competing at the first three levels, but when I got in front of the larger audience at the Conference, I froze. I allowed my internal negative voices to let fear take over. As a result I was not as powerful as I could have been. I was certainly upset with myself after that competition!

Speech competitions are nothing like conducting a speaking gig. Each speech is five to seven minutes long and initially this was a huge challenge for me because I am used to doing keynotes of an hour long, or a half to a full day training session. Now I love it. That time that I allowed fear to take over was a bone of contention for me so I re-entered the very next year. This time I did not let anything get in my way, and although I did not win the competition, I did win over the voices in my head.

Sometimes we are just competing with ourselves. I call this pushing ourselves through our comfort zone. If we are comfortable all the time, do we really grow? I think not.

Wise is the person who is willing to make a fool of themselves. They just might grow!

Influencing With Impact

Yesterday I had the wonderful opportunity to listen to a speaker from Quebec speak about Connecting with Impact. He was full of energy and very funny. Everyone in the room was learning by having fun. He spoke about being different, not being afraid to stand out, and how important our attitude is in life. I could not have agreed with him more.

He demonstrated how much one person's influence can affect the day for many people. He called on the audience for volunteers and used an example of starting your day with an upsetting event, and showed how we respond to the event is what gives us our end result.

We all know this to be true. For example, if we head off to work and someone cuts us off in traffic so that we nearly have an accident, we may not feel very good. If it was a rough start to the day at home, this secondary event just compounds our initial frustration. Here is the deal, though. It is how we respond to these events that determines how our day is going to be and how the day of those around us could potentially be as well. If you snap at the first person you meet at the office, that person thinks "What's up with her?" Then they get ticked off and pass on that anger to the next person and so on. It demonstrates how much impact one person can actually have on those around them!

But the reverse is also true. If we start each day by acknowledging and greeting those we work with by showing genuine appreciation, it is more likely to be passed along and everyone has a great day.

I know I have said this over and over again, but becoming aware of what we do, how we think, and how we feel has a huge impact on our life. How easy is it to influence someone's day? What if we consciously chose to do that every day in a positive manner? Some people may think you are crazy, but others will begin to copy you and eventually it becomes a way of life in your workplace. It is like switching from the deadly habits to caring habits.

We can all do our bit to help each other have a better day. What will you do today to help someone else have a great one today?

Is Confidence A Choice?

This morning I worked with a client who wanted to discuss her lack of confidence. As a coach I wanted to get clearer on what areas she really wanted to change so I said to her, "Explain to me what you mean by more confidence."

She went on to talk about all the areas in her life where she is lacking confidence. Her children are grown and have personal relationship issues. She somehow took this to mean she was a terrible mother and was allowing this perceived failure to crossover into her work life.

She was going to a business meeting soon with a group of her peers and she wished she could just show up with confidence. She was telling herself that she did not have much to offer, and that "everyone else" was more educated and smarter than she. I then asked her if that thought was true.

She looked at me, wide eyed, and said "No, it is not true. I really do not know." I then asked her how it served her to think that way. She agreed it did not and was amazed at how she had let herself go down that rabbit hole!

You see, what you think about you become! She is struggling with a relationship issue with one person and has given her power to that person without even realizing it. We looked at limiting beliefs, her strengths, and the times in her life where she felt confident.

She said, "I need to 'feel' it – really 'feel' the confidence." As soon as she remembered times when she had felt confident, she looked at me and said "I have it. I have the feeling back!"

Here's the thing: she had it within her the whole time. However, this is the value of working with a coach! A coach gets really curious about things and asks the questions to bring out what you already have inside.

What are you doing to invest in yourself? Have you ever thought about working with a coach? Perhaps it's time you did.

Is This Normal?

As I've said numerous times, our sex drive is the most powerful biological urge that we have within us. There is evidence of this even before birth as we can see a tiny erection in the male fetus in an ultrasound image.

In fact, if we play close attention to babies as we bath, dress, or change their diapers, we can see the presence of this urge. Often a very small baby will put their hands right on their genitals as soon as the diaper is taken off. Why? Because it feels good.

Children sometimes engage in childhood sex games and this catches many people, parents, and day care workers alike, off guard. It all depends on the amount of education we receive about sex and sexuality and development in how we respond to this activity. Children do like to play doctor!

It was not uncommon for us to receive phone calls from daycare workers, kindergarten teachers, or school counselors with questions about this subject. There was always the worry that the child must have been sexually abused. Usually with sexual abuse cases though, there are different behaviors that seem more adult related than simple curiosity.

But children checking each other out and wanting to touch each other's genitals is generally normal and curiosity based as well as fun. Masturbation is sometimes involved and this is where adults struggle the most, e.g. "What do I do when a child is masturbating in front of me?"

I need to emphasize that it is important to be aware of your own level of knowledge and comfort with this intimate subject. The best way to deal with masturbation is to acknowledge it as a natural, pleasurable experience, but to teach that it is private. Tell the child that if they feel the urge to do this, they should go to the privacy of their own bedroom. Explain that other people may feel uncomfortable seeing this happen.

There are adults today living with guilt because of the childhood sex games they played as a child, being unaware that this was normal sexual behavior of children. If at any time the sex play was forced upon them, then maybe it was abuse, but a lot of the time it is simple child sex play.

JOY

"The more I use Choice Theory, the more joy I have and the more freedom."

This is a statement that one of our participants made at a recent training I facilitated. As I was pondering about what to write this morning, this quote came to mind. It is a simple statement, but profound at the same time.

You see, it is about personal development. This quote was from someone that was truly working hard to integrate the ideas of Choice Theory into their life. The results, you might wonder? Why, more joy and more freedom!

Christmas is a very busy time of the year and sometimes we can get caught up in all the busy-ness of the season. Where do you take your joy?

Doug and I put our outdoor Christmas decorations up the latter part of November on a fairly warm day. We wanted to go all out last year because the grandchildren are now living within twenty minutes of us. Besides, I love seeing the decorations we put up at Christmas time.

We went and got ourselves a blow-up bear that looks like he is waving to you as you drive by. Doug and I enjoy him as we never quite know what he is going to do. Yes, we turn on a light switch and he fills with air, but depending on the wind, sometimes he stands on the porch and sometimes he sits on the porch! Thankfully we have him tied so he won't blow away!

Yesterday our grandchildren arrived, saw the lights and the deflated bear. They asked if we could blow him up. As he was filling with air we heard the squeals of joy from a three, five, and seven-year-old. In fact, the five-year-old stood in front of the bear and jumped up and down with a look of pure pleasure on his face. It was not such a big thing that Doug and I did with that bear, but the joy it brought our grandchildren filled our hearts so much that we will hang on to those squeals in our memories for years!

When was the last time you just squealed for the fun of it? Do you fill yourself with joy? It reminds me that in order to be able to carry on with the hustle and bustle of everyday life, we also need to fill ourselves up with activities that bring us joy! Make sure you take some time to experience your own personal joy whatever that is for you!

The More Open I Am, The Happier I Will Be

This is a lesson I learned early on in understanding the ideas of Dr. William Glasser. You see, at that time I was constantly making judgments. As a nurse, I was taught to judge. Judge the condition of my patients, judge the work of others, judge the right amount of medicine to give, etc.

I believe we make judgments, minute by minute, every day. Without being able to judge, we would not survive.

So what is judgment? According to the Oxford Dictionary:

1. *"The ability to make considered decisions or come to sensible conclusions, e.g. 'an error of judgment.'*
2. *An opinion or conclusion, e.g. 'they make subjective judgments about children's skills.'*
3. *Criticize or condemn someone from a position of assumed moral superiority."*

It is the last statement that is so important. Have you ever judged someone only to find out that you really missed the mark? The beauty of the Procedures that Lead to Change (Reality Therapy) is that we learn to communicate with people by removing ourselves and our judgments of them. How often have we heard people say things like "You'll never amount to anything" or "You can't possibly do that!"

When we learn Choice Theory, we understand that all information that we take in comes in to a place where we attach a value to it, either, neutral, positive, or negative. This is called the valuing filter. I have learned that the more open I can keep that filter the much happier I will be.

Recently I attended a seminar on diversity. The presenter spoke about the workplace, how we interact with our co-workers, and how we never know where the worker is coming from. For example, when someone gives an answer to an issue, they are always coming from their personal frame of reference. None of us have the same experiences in life and if we judge an individual by what they do and say without going deeper, we may miss a gem.

Let's look at the definition used above in the beginning of this writing. It said "an opinion or conclusion." This is probably why we get in so much trouble in our relationships. We base our opinions on what we have learned and on our own experiences. How often as teachers/parents do we judge our students capabilities? But if we could use more open ended questions and guide the child, we have no idea really what they are capable of doing.

Okay, so I have rambled a bit here. All I wanted to say is try to live a life with less judgment and see what happens. Be consciously aware when you are making such judgments and determine if they are accurate. The less you judge, the happier you will be – guaranteed. As my father could be heard saying almost daily "Judge not, want not."

Just Accept Me

"If you cannot accept me for who I am... what I do... where I live... I just don't need you in my life."

"I've been single for a while and I have to say I like who I am becoming."

These are two statements I heard recently from clients. Both are examples of personal growth in relationships. So often we get involved with someone thinking we have a lot in common and become emotionally entwined and hooked. After a few months we start to see all the qualities that are far from any picture we had in our head of what we wanted from a potential partner in the first place.

I looked at the first statement which was made by a young man. How important is it to be accepted for who you are, what you do for work, and in life, and where you live or where you have come from? For someone to make a statement like this seems to me like they have been involved with someone who wanted to change them into their own ideal mate.

This is the ultimate example of external control. Of course, keep in mind the only relationship education we receive is what we see around us. After a lifetime of working with people, I have learned trying to mold others is all too common. Someone wants to change the person they are strongly attracted to into the person they think they should be.

Can people change? Yes, they can, but only if it is satisfying a need for them to do so. Using the deadly habits of blaming, controlling, complaining, threatening, nagging, and criticizing will destroy a relationship.

In the second quote, this person has realized how important it is to be comfortable in their own skin. It is important to know that you can be happy alone or with someone. When we enter a relationship because we cannot stand the idea of being alone, we will continue to attract the type of person who we are used to having in our life. We need to become consciously aware of the kind of person we would like to share our life with, but, more importantly, to know that with or without someone we are happy with ourselves.

I have said all this before, but it is equally important to have at least one significant person in our lives that cares about us. It does not necessarily have to be a lover. It can be a good friend, family member, or someone else. Most major problems experienced in life are relationship problems. The more we can share our quality world pictures and find common matches, the happier we will be. It is also important to be able to respect the different pictures as well and accept that we do not have to like all the same things. We need to meet our own basic needs without infringing on the rights and needs of others.

Here is the bottom line: we can only receive love to the extent that we can love ourselves.

KEY TO SUCCESS

The key to success in life is not how much you know, but how self-aware you are. James Allen author of the book *As a Man Thinketh* writes "What you think about you become." Our belief system is the architect of the results we intend to become.

All learning takes place in our subconscious mind. If we think about our perceptual system and how all information passes through our sensory system, our knowledge filter and valuing filter, there are tons of learning happening of which we are totally unaware. Think about habits. Simply put, they are the children of our belief systems. Our day-to-day interactions, simple things like getting dressed or going to work are examples.

When we are not fully present, our belief system automatically generates our thoughts, feelings, and behaviors, which in turn, generate their results. Even when we understand Choice Theory, if we are not choosing to be more consciously aware, we continue to look for reasons outside of ourselves for our results. For example, you are late for work or a meeting. What is the first thing you say? It is like you are programmed to give an excuse such as "The traffic was crazy this morning," or "That construction will never end."

Now think about your personal and business goals and the results you've had in the past year. Most of us do not even think about last year's results, good and bad, only to repeat what we have always done.

Most people do not think into their results, but the top 1% of business owners understand the power of the process of getting the results they want. Bottom line: things have to change *in* you before they can change *for* you!

KIDS ARE AMAZING!

Recently my grandchildren came to visit while their mother went and got her driver's license. They wanted to play outside. They were two other little girls outside playing in their yard with a fence separating them. It was fascinating just to watch them play.

First, they all stood and looked at each other like an adult would do upon walking into a room full of strangers at a networking event. My middle grandson was not outside so the oldest one came in and got him to go out and join them. Why, you might ask? It is because he is the extroverted one in the family. Within a few minutes they were all talking to each other.

So what do five kids separated by a fence do to get along? Do they introduce themselves? No. The second grandson simply said "This is my sister and my brother. Do you want to play something?" What would they play? Doug suggested that he had a few toys in the garage from last summer they could use, so he got them out and left them alone. We watched them for quite a while to see what they'd do.

You see, humans are always figuring out ways to get their needs met and kids are no exception. In fact, these kids seemed to be pretty good at it. They started tossing a ball back and forth over the fence. Then they tossed two, three and four balls over! They got tired of doing that and started running around their individual spaces kicking soccer balls. One little girl showed my grandson how to do cartwheels and he tried to copy her. Then they tried climbing up the fence. It was too tall for any of them to actually get over it.

Suddenly the other two girls had a great idea. They got out their giant water guns and the fun began squirting each other over the fence. The whole time they were laughing and screaming and squealing. Then my middle grandson got hit right in the face with the water. Ordinarily he would have come running to me in tears! But this time, he did not want his new friends to see him cry. My laughing with him sort of helped as well. We got a towel, dried him off, and away he went again.

My three-year-old granddaughter decided she wanted to blow bubbles. This was too much for the little four-year-old on the other side of the fence. Next thing I knew, she was asking her mother if she could come and visit in our yard. Both little girls made their way over. They all found a space under the trees at the back of the yard where they could build a fort! All in all my grandchildren said they had a really great time at Grammy Mo's place! All Grammy Mo did was let them be kids and use their own creativity to have fun. I really enjoyed watching all the antics and could not wait to write about this day for you.

When was the last time you tapped into your own creativity? You see, we all have everything we need inside of us. Do we stop and take the time to really play? If not, we should.

Know Your Worth

I came across this wonderful quote from Les Brown who also suggested that we shoot for the moon and we may land on a star. What a wonderful speaker he is!

> *"Know your worth! Do not fall into the trap of believing that who you are and what you are worth are dependent on who you are with or what you have. No one can ever give you your self-worth. You decide if you let someone rob you of it. Become aware of how you medicate the pain in your life. It may include food, shopping, alcohol, drugs, or relationships which continue to diminish your sense of self."*

> *"You will never truly feel good until you learn to love yourself unconditionally. Your life is a gift. Say to yourself constantly... 'I deserve the best that life has to offer.' Live from this place. Make it a point to build new relationships that are positive, encouraging and supportive. Take it upon yourself to develop a sense of purpose, optimism, discipline. Realize that no one can take away your most valuable assets – your mind and your self-esteem, without your permission. You have GREATNESS within you!"*
>
> – Les Brown

Every once in a while I think it is important that we step back and take a look at how we are treating ourselves. I think this quote is one that we could all post on a wall somewhere to remind ourselves that we do deserve the best that life has to offer! Stop and think about what is your purpose and your own inner greatness.

I love that Les says no one can give you your self-worth and you decide if you are going to get someone rob you of it. I have talked before about three little words in the English language with big meaning. I speak about how we are taught from a very early age not to be **selfish** and to share with others. Sometimes this is reinforced so much that we lose sight of ourselves and we give and give and give until we have nothing left and we become **self-less**. Take these words of Les Brown and remind yourself you need to stop every now and then, take stock, and fill yourself (become **self-full**) up so you can serve others.

What are you doing for yourself today?

Language of Choice

This past weekend I was the "test" speaker for the Division E Toastmaster's Evaluation Contest. What that means is I do a speech and then receive feedback from the contestants. This feedback is designed to help me grow as a speaker.

As a public speaker, and a member of Toastmasters International, I jumped at the chance to receive such feedback. This is the best way to grow as a speaker.

Some of the responses I received were on my choice of words I used in my speech. One such word was the word "frustrating." Since learning Control Theory and later Choice Theory, I realized how using "ing" has become an integral part of my vocabulary.

I was describing the day my computer died and said "As I was frustrating, I continued to try to solve the issue." It was brought to my attention that maybe I could have used the phrase "I was frustrated" and it would have been less confusing.

I appreciated their comments because it brought an awareness that I need to have when speaking to my audience. I rarely use such phrases as I was frustrated, depressed, because they indicate that something happened to me.

My belief is that I always have a choice in the behaviors I choose. Words like frustrated, depressed, guilty, anxious are all static words. In the words of Dr. William Glasser in his book *Take Charge of Your Life*:

"By transforming these static words into actions that more accurately reflect choices, I hope to imply that these behaviors are subject to change. As you transform your life using a choice theory point of view, you will see that this use of language helps to keep your thoughts more flexible.

This transition will not be easy. Lifelong beliefs, especially if they are held by almost everyone you know, die hard." I became acutely aware at how I now could choose to explain my choice of language, and have since practiced this theory in my daily speaking. What words are you using in your conversations?

LET'S TALK PLEASURE

Dr. Christiane Northrup suggests that as women we are constantly looking over our shoulder for the pleasure police because we have been taught that anything pleasurable is suspect. I dare say some men would do that too, depending on the messages we have received and accepted when it comes to pleasure.

Look at some of the things we say aloud that inform us about our beliefs around experiencing pleasure Here are just a few phrases we say to ourselves:

GUILTY PLEASURES
SINFULLY DELICIOUS
WAY TOO MUCH FUN
DROP-DEAD GORGEOUS
DIE LAUGHING

How often do we use these phrases? Can you permit yourself to indulge in what brings you pleasure? We have already discussed the effect of negativity on our cells in our body and how we can become ill. Depriving ourselves of pleasure is not conducive to alleviating stress and inflammation.

Do not hold back from experiencing pleasure. Be direct and not apologetic when it comes to seeking it. Know and ask for what you enjoy, want, and deserve. Don't settle for what you think should be enough. As Dr. Northrup says "if you want to spend the entire evening watching junk TV and giving yourself a pedicure instead of going to a community meeting you said you would attend purely out of a sense of obligation, go for it."

I confess it took me a very long time to give myself permission to enjoy life's little pleasures and an even longer time for the bigger ones, but what I have learned is the more pleasure I experience, the easier it is to deal with the negativity that comes into my life.

As I have said for a long time, "We need to fill ourselves up in order to be able to continue to give to others." Make a list of all the little things that can bring you pleasure. It could be as simple as a nice, long soak in the tub or opening a door for a breath of fresh air. Go for it.

Life Is Over At Fifteen

This is another one of those heart-wrenching stories from my years working in Sexual Health. One Monday morning, a young woman skipped school and came to see me at the center. She was very upset. She had been dating a young man for about three months at this point.

She told him she believed she was too young to have sex and wanted to wait until she was older, and he had told her that he was okay with her decision. On the previous weekend they had been out with friends and having a good time. She and her boyfriend were very close. He was pressuring her to have sex with him and she did not want to. She explained that she loved him, but she was not ready for sex. He continued to pressure her.

She told me the next thing she knew was that they had engaged in sex against her will. She felt terrible. She really believed that he loved her and that she somehow was hurting him by not wanting to have sex.

Monday morning she realized she had been a victim of date rape. Her wise girlfriend had suggested she go to the clinic. Through lots of tears she shared her story with me. She exclaimed with tears streaming down her face, "My life is over! Now that this has happened, I might as well have sex with everyone and I want birth control! I suppose I need to be checked for STD's!!" She was angry as well.

As I talked with her, I decided to ask her some questions about her quality world pictures of her first experience of sex. She described how she would have been with her partner for more than a year and that they would be totally committed to each other. They would have birth control in place and that he would be checked for sexually transmitted diseases. She wanted them to be in a comfortable place with soft music and candlelight, and they would be truly treating each other in a loving way. She was very clear on what she wanted her first sexual experience to be like.

After she described all this, I looked at her and said "So was the experience you had on the weekend like the picture you just described?"

Sobbing, she said "No! That is why my life is over!" I looked at her and said, "So the picture you have of your first sexual experience the way you want it has not happened yet, has it?" She looked at me with an astonished look on her face and replied, "What do you mean... yet?" "Well, did you have control in this situation? Was it the way you wanted it to be?" I asked her. "No." I then asked her, "Could you still wait to get your first time the way you want it?" She looked at me and a small smile emerged on her beautiful face. She realized her life was not over and that she still had a choice.

She believed that if you have sex once you might as well have it with whomever because life was over! Where did that limiting belief come from? We all have that strong biological urge within us. We need to learn how to manage it. She did continue for counseling for a while after that first session and she did hang on to her original picture.

We never know when we say something to someone how that might influence their life!

Look At You!

"Look at you! Look at your energy! We can tell you are doing your passion!" I have been thinking about those words since my day finished yesterday. You see, I cannot do all that I want to do and I am aware of this fact. I have been working on keeping the main thing the main thing. In other words, what are my goals for the year and am I focused on them, or am I letting myself get distracted. For example, I take some new training and now I am able to teach this new training, but my goal is to continue to teach Choice Theory. If I go off and start preparing to teach something else that is not necessarily my passion, I am removing myself from my main focus.

You see, I am just like a crow that is attracted to shiny objects. I have become mindful of my own capacity and what I cannot only physically do, but also what brings me true meaning. I am capable of doing many things, but just because I can do something doesn't mean I should nor want to do it. It is so easy to want to be everything to everyone. This is why priorities have to be set – to avoid overtaxing one's self.

My coach has been constantly driving home the importance of keeping "the main thing the main thing." For that reason I will be letting go of a number of things that I do and will be looking for outside help to accomplish other things that I need help doing.

Are there jobs/responsibilities that you are hanging on to that are not need satisfying, or do not feed your spirit by adding meaning to your life? What can you shed?

You know the first time I had to look at this was when my son was three-years-old and I was an on call nurse in the operating room. I could be called back anytime for an emergency and I was taking on all the responsibility for the house cleaning, dishes, laundry, etc. My response to this was to hire a housekeeper. Sometimes we think we cannot afford such a luxury, but I am here to tell you that you cannot afford not to if you want to enjoy some down time.

I still have housekeepers thirty-six years later. It is simply the cost of two evenings a month out. In business, it is a similar thing. As entrepreneurs, we think it is cheaper to do everything ourselves, but is it really? Is it working towards our strengths when we do that? Besides, in both of these cases you are actually providing someone else with a job.

What jobs can you give to someone else? How would it enhance your life to do so? What are you waiting for?

Love Or Power And Control?

This is another story about a student being referred for relationship counseling with me because her friends, parents, and school counselor were worried about her. She had been dating a young man for a little over a year and wanted to break up with him, but she was afraid to do that because she was scared he would kill himself.

We talked about relationships and I asked her to evaluate hers against the following questions:

Love And Belonging
Do I feel loved and like I belong with this person?
Do I believe they love me no matter what or is it conditional love?
Are we truly close?
Do I think and feel like they care about me and what happens to me?
Can I count on this person to be there for both the good and bad times?

Power
Do I feel in control of myself in this relationship?
Do I understand that the only person I can control is myself?
Does my partner understand the same thing?
Do I feel important in this relationship?
Do I feel respected and listened to?

Fun
Do I enjoy myself with this person?
Do I laugh with my partner?
Do I learn new things with my partner?
Do I play with my partner?
Am I adventurous with my partner?

FREEDOM

Do I share with my partner?

Do I feel independent in my relationship?

Do I make some of the decisions about what we do?

Am I free to be creative?

Do I feel free to say yes or no?

She was able to evaluate that her relationship was not at all good, and recognized that it was all about power and control. The problem was her boyfriend kept telling her that he was going to kill himself if she broke up with him. He would show up at her house at night and cry outside her bedroom window that he would kill himself until her father caught him and asked him to leave.

She wanted to take responsibility for him. We talked about whose behavior she could control and she understood that she could only control her own. At the same time I asked her whose behavior her boyfriend could control and she agreed his own, but realized she was letting him control her as well. She needed a plan.

She decided that she would talk with her boyfriend's best friend and his parents, and tell them when she was going to break up with him so they could be with him to get him the help he needed. She was able to do this and the young man eventually ended up getting some counseling. They were both doing the best they could do with what they knew.

LOVE – A VICTORY MARCH

Hallelujah by Leonard Cohen is a love song. "Love is not a victory march," he says, "It's a cold and it's a broken Hallelujah."

Life's like that, too. Our successes are public, but behind closed doors everybody has their difficult times.

The happiest couples you know have faced real private struggles. The business people you think of as being a total success regularly face failure and moments of fear and vulnerability.

Love is not a victory march reminded me of Dr. Glasser and Carleen in their book *Getting Together and Staying Together*, where Dr. Glasser says not too long after you are married, someone invariably asks, "Is the honeymoon over yet?" What they are really saying is "Have the power struggles begun?"

I believe the other statements are true as well. I do think though that love is a behavior we choose. Through all our private struggles, failures, etc., we can still choose loving behaviors towards one another. But we need to be consciously aware that it is a choice.

Many of us grew up in externally controlled environments so we accept that "She made me angry," or "I hit her/him because they made me do it." Nobody makes you do anything. It is always you who chooses your behavior. Tough words, I know, but if we simply practice the caring habits regardless of what the other person does, life will be easier.

LOVE, DR. DYER

On August 30, 2015, we lost another great man of this lifetime, Dr. Wayne Dyer. This is a man whose writings I have followed since my son was very young. One of his many books *What Do Children Want?* was very helpful to me as a young parent, and in recent years I have often thought about how influences like his writing have affected me. I think I found some tools in that first book to help me be a better parent which led me to Dr. Glasser's work. Reflecting about it, it was a natural fit as both men spoke to me in their writing.

I am feeling so blessed to have heard Dr. Dyer speak in Moncton last May. Knowing that two years previous he had been battling leukemia, I opted to buy the more expensive seats so I could sit right at his feet at the front of the stage where he was sitting. This is a behavior that I would rarely choose, but that experience gave me a very special gift – a gift of love.

I was able to spend a few minutes with Dr. Dyer and speak with him about some struggles I was having in making some decisions about my life's direction, namely feeling pulled in many directions at the same time. He simply looked at me and said it is about "LOVE." As I walked away, I thought "He is correct. It really is about love." From that moment, I think into whether I can love what I am asked to do before making a decision and a commitment. It has greatly simplified my life.

That night he spoke for three hours. If you have an opportunity to listen to that presentation, you will not regret it. It was called "I Am." He emphasized that all we have is this present moment, so true to what Dr. Glasser was saying years ahead of him.

Interestingly, he ended up endorsing one of Dr. Glasser's books and he was so happy about Dr. Dyer doing that. They were two like-minded men supporting each other, loving what they do, and sharing it with the world. Now they are our angels helping us to carry their legacy forward.

What are you doing that you love? Do you love daily? An article written by a friend about alcoholics stated that all they need is love, but most of the time, they are treated with hate, resentment, etc.

Love is all around us. Sending love out to you today!

Man's Search For Meaning

If you have not read Victor Frankl's book *Man's Search for Meaning*, I can assure you that if you should choose to do so, it will inspire you to find significance in the very act of living.

Psychiatrist Victor Frankl's memoir has riveted generations of readers with his description of life in the Nazi death camps, as well as his lessons for spiritual survival. In his book he says, "We cannot avoid suffering but we can choose how to cope with it, find meaning in it and move forward."

Dr. Glasser often referred to the works of Frankl. This book has been recently republished and I ordered a copy. I will share one snippet with you so you'll get a sense of the story. The book is not very long, in very large print, and easy to read.

He writes: "One evening when we were already resting on the floor of our hut, dead tired, soup bowls in hand, a fellow prisoner rushed in and asked us to run out into the assembly grounds and see the wonderful sunset. Standing outside we saw sinister clouds glowing in the west and the whole sky alive with clouds of ever-changing shapes and colors, from steel blue to blood red. The desolate grey mud huts provided a sharp contrast, while the puddles on the muddy ground reflected the glowing sky. Then, after minutes of moving silence, one prisoner said to another, how beautiful the world **could** be!"

You see, even in the concentration camps, people chose to look for the positive. Sometimes we complain that we cannot be positive, but look around you. There is always something positive with every negative thing around us.

Dr. John Demartini, author of *The Breakthrough Experience*, teaches that the world is in perfect balance. He says when we are buried in the negativity, we are not consciously aware of the positive around us and vice versa. When everything is positive in our lives, we are unconscious to all the negativity around us. It is what we are consciously aware of at the time.

Can we choose to be more consciously aware? Think about this the next time you are mired down in misery!

March Madness

As you may or may not know I am a huge basketball fan. Yes, I was probably one of the first people in line to buy tickets when we got our own National Basketball Team here in Moncton, and I have been a season ticket holder ever since. Our local team has had a tough year. First of all the owner decided to move back to New York, and a manager from Ontario came in and took over.

He did start a booster club, which helped a little, but attendance fell off. You see the owner, while living here, made sure the season ticket holders were informed of everything that was happening through-out the year and special offers were made to ticket holders first. Accordingly, the fan base kept growing.

Then the owner lost a parent and with a young toddler, she was drawn home to New York to be with her family. She told us what an agonizing decision that was for her, leaving her basketball family here and going to her family back home. Consequently, rumors started to spread about the sale of the team, etc., and morale plummeted.

The players were not really in the game. You could almost imagine that they were not sure where they would be next season. Then injuries plagued the team. These are not excuses, but one can easily see how the team and the crowd's morale would start to dwindle, and it did. The team lost a lot of games, but only by single digits. The fans started fading away. It was not a particularly good season.

So what do you do when you are down? Do you dig deep inside and do the best you can, or do you just adopt a give up attitude? These players had a great season, all things considered, and when it came to the play-offs they dug in and won over the number one seed team in the first play-off game. They proved they could do it, but their win was not to be repeated. Soon the season ended for them.

Leadership is key! The coach had his first chance to be head coach and even was named Coach of the Week once by the league during the season, but with the leadership in flux, there is not much evidence of strong support. I may be mistaken in my assumptions, as I am looking at it from the sidelines and sharing my personal experience.

In order to be successful in the future, the team members will need a leader they are willing to follow so that they can be leaders in their job. Where are you leading the way? Do you recognize it?

MENTALLY CHALLENGED

I had an interesting conversation with someone in our inner circle about services for children who are mentally challenged. We discussed the benefits and drawbacks to integration of these special needs children with the general school population.

It reminded me of my youth. When I was in High School, mentally challenged youth went to a separate school. I used to volunteer there at the end of my regular school day. They were such a joy to work with and to this day I've stayed in touch with a couple of them.

One such person is John. When my father passed away a few years ago, the first person to knock on my door was John. It brought tears to my eyes when he looked at me and said, "They told me he is gone. Can I come in?" I invited him in and we sat at dining room table with a cup of tea. He was very talkative. While listening to him, I was in awe at how much he was actually talking, so I said to him, "John, you are talking a lot. I don't ever remember you talking very much." He looked at me and said "My father died and now I have to talk." I was very tearful. I thought to myself how sad it was that he never talked because someone talked for him. Today we would call this an enabling behavior.

One of the beautiful ideas of understanding Choice Theory, the needs, the total behavior, the creative system and the quality world, is we can use that understanding with everyone we work with including the mentally challenged. The tools we have are for everyone! The procedures that lead to change are the best communication tools available and are very powerful with working with this group of people. I can't help but wonder if we had been aware of this way back when if John's life would have turned out better. If he had been asked about his quality world pictures, what might have been the different? I know he was loved and cared for and certainly seems happy now.

What a gift we all have received from learning these ideas.

Mmm... A Cigarette!

Oh the power of Quality World pictures! We are taught to be careful what we put into our Quality World as need satisfying, especially when it comes to addictive substances!

Our Quality World is that tiny space in our head where we store the pictures of people, places, things, values and beliefs that are important to us. We behave to get that quality world picture and when we get it one of more of our needs will be met.

Let me give you a quick example. Our new kitchen is very much in my Quality World. I want a kitchen that is less cluttered and more serviceable, one that will help us remain in our current location for a longer period of time. If I look at the needs that will be satisfied, there will be survival, so I won't have to get on my painful knees because I will have bottom drawers instead of cupboards. It will be less cluttered because we will now have a portable island. Our table and chairs will be gone plus the garbage bin will be hidden, so I anticipate a certain sense of freedom. Our power needs will be met when we stand back and admire all we went through to manage this project.

So where am I going with this? Today I decided to take a quick trip to the dollar store for some last minutes supplies. I had a good time meeting people I knew and the line-up was not bad either. As I left the store two employees were outside taking a break and enjoying a cigarette. My first thought was "Oh no! Not more smoke to walk through!" But as I approached them, their spirits were high and they were laughing and obviously having a good time. I had one sniff of the cigarette and it took me to the Quality World picture of myself enjoying cigarettes over thirty-five years ago. Just the smell and the thought of fun brought me back to that place when after work my friends and I would go to a local café, sit and enjoy a smoke together and hash over our day.

"Wow," I thought to myself. "That was fun and very need satisfying." By the time I reached my car, I was reminding myself that was then and today we know so much more about the dangers of smoking cigarettes! Interesting just how powerful a picture like that can be. I know that I will never smoke again, but I am also very aware that it is still a choice, one that is in the best interest of my health. In other words, my picture of me living longer in good health overrides the desire to smoke again.

For a brief moment, though, I enjoyed the memory!

More Sex Talk

Really, when I think about talking about sex, I see it as one of those areas in our life where we truly need to look at our own values around the subject.

Since reproduction is part of the survival need, we are born with the necessity to reproduce. Without it we would not exist as a society. However, we have a responsibility to teach our youth about this need and how to best handle it.

Are you equipped to talk about sex with your youth? Do you have any limiting beliefs around the subject of sex? Where did you get your sex education? Do you know where to search to get reliable information?

When I entered nursing school many years ago, I did not even have the proper terminology for our sexual anatomy, so you can imagine the huge learning curve I experienced when I was hired as the first nurse to start the Reproductive Health Clinics that would later become the Sexual Health Centers in my area.

I quickly got past any limiting beliefs I might have had and learned all I could about the subject. I helped hundreds of parents and youth over the next twenty-five plus years after nursing school. I guess what I'm saying here is if I can learn about sex, so can you.

Why do we have hang-ups about the subject? Why do we feel embarrassed to talk with our kids when it is such a natural part of our body? Is this one of those beliefs that we unconsciously pick up and let it hold us back?

What's the big deal? Today talking freely about sex is more important than ever. The most important thing that you can do for your child is teach them about your values so they have a reference point to start from.

Tell them about your beliefs about early sexual activity, about unintended pregnancy, and relationships in general.

Our Life Experiences Help Us Grow!

It was 1985 and the Reproductive Health Clinic where I worked had been open for two years. It was a quiet day when a knock came on my door and the secretary said I had someone who wanted to talk with me.

I looked up and saw a tall handsome man in his thirties who seemed extremely nervous. I asked him how I could help him. He stammered and stuttered a little and said that he had been looking for someone to talk with for over a year and that what he wanted to discuss was extremely personal. All my training had taught me to reassure him that everything we talked about would be confidential.

Finally, tearfully, he opened up and told me that he had been diagnosed HIV positive a year earlier and had spent the last year just wandering around wondering what to do. Keep in mind that the date was 1985. HIV/AIDS was just beginning to become known in the medical community. We knew enough that it was a killer.

This is one of those challenges that you are trained to handle on an intellectual level, but when it comes to an emotional level it is a whole different kettle of fish. I don't mind saying I was terrified. I felt myself wanting to push my chair back away from him, yet intellectually I knew I was not in danger. My heart went out to him and I wondered how he found me as I stayed in my seat.

He said that the word around town was that those nurses at the Reproductive Clinic were really nice to talk to, seemed to truly care, and could keep things confidential. I am able to write this now because eventually his confidentiality became very public. At that time, I did not have my Reality Therapy Training, but I think looking back that it must have been very much a part of me.

As we chatted, he told me he just did not know what to do. The medical profession had no idea how to deal with him, and, in fact, he sensed that they were all scared of him. The more we talked, the more frustrated he became. He had been doing lots of research himself, but was dismayed by the lack of services in our community. Finally, drawing on all I knew at that time, I looked at him and said "It seems to me you have two choices. You can live with this, or you can die with it. Which is it going to be?" He sat quietly for a few minutes, looked at me, and said strongly, "I am going to live with it! Who can I talk to within the health department to push for community services to help those dealing with this condition?"

Eventually a group of community people came together because of his resolve and SIDA/AIDS Moncton was born. I learned so much from this man. The first lesson was to trust my intellect. The second lesson was how to decorate a platter for a Christmas party. (He loved to do this sort of thing.) The third lesson and the most powerful one was that in fact, ONE PERSON CAN MAKE A DIFFERENCE!

Several years later he did die from AIDS, but not without influencing an entire community with better services both for prevention and treatment.

Today, every Christmas, I have a little white angel that I place near the top front of my Christmas tree to remind me of him! He was a wonderful man and I know he is one of my many angels standing over me.

People Change When You Grow

I have the good fortune to belong to an Entrepreneur Mastery Inner Circle with some great entrepreneurs from around the world. This is one of the joys that the invention of the internet makes possible.

One of the threads in our online forum is about personal growth. One individual said he is growing so much he is finding that his own personal circle is changing. He asked the rest of us to share our experiences on this subject.

He talked about how people who used to be in his life irritate him now and how even people close to him don't seem to understand him anymore. He wanted to know if others have experienced the same sort of happening in their life.

I shared one of my many stories that I will share with you here.

Back in the mid '80s I was the first nurse hired to run the Sexual Health Center in our province.

This was a huge area of struggle for me. My entire life changed. The more I learned and the more I understood, the further away I got from a lot of people in my life. It was a real roller coaster of emotions. There was a lot of rejection because of the subject material I was teaching etc., but I was growing and did not want to stop the process.

For a long time I felt guilty for studying, learning, and growing. Over time I came to understand that if we never grow, nothing changes. In terms of my relationships at the time, I was growing and changing, but many of the people around me were not and my relationships changed. Many of those people are no longer in my life.

I probably served thousands of people in our community. For years in that position I did over fifty speaking engagements annually for parents and youth alike. I was interviewed on TV and in the press. I was nowhere near the person I had been at the beginning of accepting this job.

So yes, when we learn and develop personally, the people around us change. Some for the better and some just dwindle away from us. And sometimes we become impatient. It can be extremely frustrating trying to have a conversation with someone who is on a different level than you.

The other piece of learning I discovered with my personal growth and development is that there will always be naysayers, the people that want to hold you back or knock you down. Nowadays I simply seek out the supporters.

This having been said, I would not change a thing about that experience. How about you? Would you change anything after learning what you know today?

PERCEPTIONS

Today I write about a great lesson I learned from my coach and a member of an Inner Circle Mastermind that I belong to. You see last week he shared an e-mail about someone he had an interaction with over the use of his services.

He shared his interaction with a rather scathing and off the wall person. It would have been hilariously funny if I had not known the person he was writing about. Or did I know this person?

You see, he named the person and with the copy/paste function he was able to post verbatim what he had said to him. There was even some foul language. I was in shock, to say the least.

I read on and the e-mails went back and forth. I could not believe my eyes. You know when you think you know people, sometimes their behavior can really be very different than you would ever expect from them.

But here's the thing. Was I being consciously aware of my perceptions or was I being hauled into a not so nice story? Well, I have to admit at the time it was kind of fun.

But as I stepped back and really thought about it, the person I know would never had written those emails using such poor grammar. He is an author after all. There were other indicators as well that this was not him. The swearing in the emails and the use of external control were indicators of that.

How often do you check your perceptions? How often does someone say or do something and you just take it as being real?

Getting back to the story, I thought about this person I knew. I looked him up on Facebook and the internet, and what I found just did not match with this email being shared by my colleague.

What I did find was that there were about twenty other persons with the exact same name, so this story could have been about any of them. I spoke with another colleague about the email I received and she agreed it was not the person I had originally thought it was about.

So what did I learn? What have you learned so far?

Be careful what you say in an email as you never know who will see it and what they will do with it.

How quickly a person's reputation can be ruined, even though they have done nothing.

I am going to check out my own name online more regularly to see if there is anything slanderous being posted against someone with a name the same as mine. I already know there are a number of Maureen McIntosh's so technically it could happen.

The biggest lesson I learned is to think critically and always check your perceptions before jumping to conclusions!

Performance Reviews

Recently, I had the wonderful opportunity to attend a Human Resource event where the subject was performance reviews. When the presenter asked the audience how many people liked doing reviews, only a couple out of ninety participants raised their hands. When asked how many employees like getting reviews, no hands went up.

There was a great deal of discussion on the subject. There were commentaries made on what the performance reviews looked like, while others talked about how the rating system of 1-5 could be useless. Some discussed how performance reviews were the same year after year. They talked about how often performance reviews are done and about who did the reviews.

Then the subject of compensation came up as a possible reward for an employee receiving a good review. It struck me how we are still very much about rewarding someone in an attempt to control them. It reminded me of my working days in the healthcare system. At one point management had started a rewards based program where if we exceeded expectations, we would be rewarded with a pay increase. Our manager told us right up front that no one in our department would get an "exceeds expectations" review which we all accepted because we understood that it was about the quality of the work, not the money.

What happened though was interesting. People began to focus on the money and who got what compensation. There was a woman who did get an "exceeds expectations" in one of the other offices and received a pay raise. We all did the same job, but she got a raise. Can you imagine what that did for the morale of our department?

Don't get me wrong. I think performance reviews are important and should be done on an ongoing basis throughout the year. The review should also contain the element of self-evaluation, because after all, who knows the work better than the worker. Have you ever received a review by a manager who did not even know what you did on a daily basis?

Bottom line? Performance reviews are done to help the worker become better and move forward with their goals. There should be an element of coaching involved which really is about asking great questions and getting the person to evaluate what they want and whether their current behavior is getting them it. Once again, it is almost always about relationships.

Purpose

"Until thought is linked with purpose, there can be no significant achievement."

– Christian Simpson

This is a quote that arrived in my inbox today. Since I'm often talking about bringing our behavior into our conscious awareness, I thought I would share it with you.

Are you living into your purpose? Do you even think about purpose? What is purpose anyway?

So many people seem to struggle with this, yet we do a lot of things on purpose every day. We get dressed, or not, on purpose. We go to work, or not, on purpose. We drive our car on purpose, so purpose can be as big or as little as we want that word to be. Are these statements true? Are you truly on purpose, or are these statements about being on autopilot?

According to Meriam Webster Free Dictionary, purpose is:

> *"something set up as an object or end to be attained;*
> *intention, resolution, determination;*
> *a subject under discussion or an action in course of execution;*
> *on purpose;*
> *by intent;*
> *intentionally*

So when people talk about living into their purpose, what are they really saying? I think the real question is are you doing what you love to do, and are you doing it with a purpose in mind? What is your picture of being on purpose?

If thought is not linked with purpose, there can be no significant achievement. Think about it. This is a true statement. We can go through life on autopilot, or we can start linking our thinking to our acting. We should frequently check how we are feeling, what is happening in our body (physiology), and pay attention to whether we are living on purpose or not.

We can't always get what we want, but we can get some of what we need.

RELATIONSHIP BAGGAGE

The other day I stumbled upon an article about unpacking relationship baggage. As I read the article I could not help but notice how negative it seemed. You see, when one carries relationship baggage, the baggage is negative from the point of view that it must contain unhappy memories about past relationships.

As I pondered that, I wondered if it would not be more worthwhile if we could empower others to dump the baggage before beginning the next relationship. Could it be better to have a clear picture of what a great relationship could look like?

Then my quirky mind took me to actually unpacking my physical baggage from my suitcase and the behaviors I choose when unpacking. If I have clean clothes in my bags, I hang on to them and put them away to wear at a later time. So when it comes to the unhappy relationship, one could hang on to what is good and save those things for their tool-box, or add them to their pictures of good relationships.

Next, while unpacking my bag, I take the dirty clothes and put them in the hamper to be washed and dried. Think about the relationship baggage. In this case, some things are bad, but a lot has been learned from this experience. It is possible to have a thorough look at the situation and determine what part one had in this relationship and "wash" themselves clean of negative behaviors and create a new behavior to use in a new relationship. For instance, getting defensive in a discussion when one could just listen and respond in a careful way without losing their temper.

Then there are the toiletries that one uses over and over again. There are the favorite toothpaste, combs, make-up, deodorant, etc. These things are the habits that occur daily that an individual feels pretty good about.

So how does one use the positives in one's lives? These are things that are important to us. Here is an opportunity to think about what one truly likes and what is non-negotiable, as well as what one would be willing to compromise on in a new relationship. It comes down to knowing what someone values and believes which I believe can be linked to compatibility.

In poor relationships, sometimes people give up things they really enjoy doing because their partner may not like doing it. But if they do too much compromising, eventually when the infatuation wears off, resentment will set in, and unhappiness comes along because one is no longer enjoying the things they like to do.

Sometimes in our suitcase we have souvenirs or memories of our trip that remind us of the good times. There will always be behaviors or other things that remind us of past experiences, but when I unpack my suitcase if there is something that no longer serves me, I throw it away. We need to maintain our awareness of this decision.

Try and remember to keep the good and discard the bad when you're looking at your relationship baggage.

Retirement

I took a trip down memory lane yesterday! I attended an open house for Support to Single Parents. This program is closing after serving our community since 1983. Nancy Hartling has been the executive director of this organization since its inception and has done a fabulous job.

However, sometimes things have to change. Nancy is ready for retirement and they were unable to secure funding for their programs to keep everyone working. Being as creative as she is, she found homes for all the programs that they offer to the community.

Sometimes we can see the cup as half empty or half full. We could view this situation as disastrous or joyful. It is both in a sense. While the programs found new homes, I am not sure about the staff. Some of them are taking their programs into their private practice. This will be a new learning curve for them.

There is always one thing in life we can be sure of and that is change. Retirement is one of those changes. In the 1800's, retirement was developed so that people could rest a few months before dying. This was at the age of 65. Today people start retiring in their mid-fifties with a life expectancy of another 25 years! This is incredible when you think about it.

In today's world, we are carving out a different future. I like to say I earned my graduation from my full-time job and then created my dream job.

Do you think about retirement? Do you have a plan?

To simply retire with no plans can create a lot of hardship. Dare to dream and set yourself up to succeed at whatever you want to do!

Standing For What Is Important!

I have been thinking a lot about leadership lately and how to become more effective in these types of roles. Leadership is not about having a title. Great leaders lead in such a way that people want to follow them. So what does it take for people to want to follow a leader? I am reminded of the work of Dr. William Glasser, who after spending time with W. Edwards Deming, a leadership guru, came up with what he perceived as the difference between a Boss and a Lead Manager.

A Boss Manager Does The Following:

Tells people what to do.

Evaluates other's behavior.

Coerces people by saying things like, "If you don't do this you will get that."

Based on external control.

Does politics.

Assigns teams and groups.

Talks the walk.

Blames others.

Directs. In other words, tells others what to do.

Creates fear.

Focuses on the past.

"It's my way or the highway." Believes that their way is the best way.

Defends.

You! There is very little "we" in the Boss Manager environment.

A Lead Manager Does The Following:

Leads concurrent evaluation. In other words, works with others to help them evaluate their behavior.

Intends no harm.

Based on Choice Theory, understands that all behavior is purposeful, and that the only behavior they can control is their own.

Centered in principles and beliefs.

Facilitates Choice Theory by involving team members and seeks input from others.

Walks the walk and talks the talk.

Admits mistakes, fixes them, and moves on. Focuses on the solution, not the problem.

Guides others.

Builds trust by sharing and seeking input from others.

Builds on today and the future.

Seeks win-win.

Seeks first to understand.

"We" is important.

If people believe they have a voice, are respected and listened to, and that the leader has their best interests at heart, they will want to do quality work for and with that person.

What kind of leader are you?

PROCRASTINATION

Procrastination is a subject at the top of my list today. You might say I am the queen of procrastination. I have been planning to de-clutter my bookshelves now for well over six months. Even though it is a choice to do it or not, once a decision was made to do so, I immediately went into procrastination mode. I knew it had to be done to make space for new and I wanted it done, but I kept putting it off.

This behavior reminded of me of studying for tests in school. I nearly always put it off until the last minute. At work, if I had a big presentation to do, I would put that off to the last minute as well. At least now when it comes to presentations, I have adopted the habit of planning ahead.

Along time ago, a wise friend told me that procrastination is another term for being a "perfectionist" who puts everything off to the last minute because then they know it can't be done perfectly! That statement has stuck with me ever since. You see, I had a picture in my head of how I wanted to organize my books, but I knew it was going to take a lot of time and a lot of work. I also love my books and I wanted the ones I was getting rid of to go to someone that would really appreciate them.

When I said I was going to organize my bookshelves this past Saturday, I had a colleague who said with a big smile and much enthusiasm "Let me help you!" She did not come and help, but she came and carried the excess away! She has a huge array of books and will add my books to her shelves where others can go and borrow them. I finally did the books, re-organized my closet and the rest of the space in that room! Phew! A big personal goal accomplished for this quarter.

As someone who chooses to procrastinate, the only way I knew I would get this done was if I put it on my list of goals for this quarter of the year. I am actually ahead by one month so am feeling quite accomplished this morning. There is a lightness in my step today, and as I walk into that room, I am looking forward to enjoying my reading and reflection space once again.

Do you procrastinate? Do you sometimes ask yourself, what you have been waiting for? Do you recognize that when you do the thing you have been putting off, there is an immediate sigh of relief and even a bounce in your step?

What is stopping you from going and doing that thing right now?

Humour In Crisis

"My attitude has always been, if you fall flat on your face, at least you're moving forward," he said. "All you have to do is get back up and try again. At least I'm practicing what I preach – though a little too literally!"

– Richard Branson

This was a quote by Richard Branson, the billionaire founder of Virgin Group when he found himself landing face first on the road, badly injuring himself as he flew over the handle bar of his bicycle while going at a high speeds training for a race. He said he saw his life pass in front of him and thought he was going to die!

Seriously. Have you ever fallen flat on your face, metaphorically? Sometimes even the best laid plans go south. How we deal with it is the key, and it's all about attitude.

I watched a video recently of John C. Maxwell preaching at Christ Fellowship Church. He was using a music stand for his bible and his notes. The stand kept collapsing and they brought him another one which collapsed as well.

He took it all in stride and made a great humorous talk out of it. It is all about attitude. He could have very easily become frustrated, but he chose to express his frustration through humor. At one point he even grabbed his water bottle and took a drink, as if to say "I need a drink!" His audience was in stitches. How different it could have been if he had chosen a different behavior.

It takes real skill to go through those rough patches with a sense of humor. In Richard Branson's case, the first person on the scene happened to be his assistant. He looked at her and said, "At least I am still alive and the good news is you still have a job!" At his most painful time, he still used humor.

Do you see the funny side of things, even when they are difficult?

I Am An Alcoholic

This morning I was following an interesting thread on Facebook about labels and how we label ourselves and others. It reminded me of a time I was invited into the school classroom to speak with a group of fourteen-year-old youths about sex. At that time my label was Sexual Health Nurse.

When I entered the room one of the young people said, "Ah, the sex nurse is here today!" My son happened to be in that class. (Can you imagine having your mother teach you about sex in front of your peers?) Anyway, I digress. The teacher became upset with that student and said, "Don't call her that!" to which my son responded, "Why not? That is who she is!"

At that moment and time I was perceived by most in the room as the "Sex Nurse" and by times I still get called by that label, but that is all it is a label. It gives me permission to talk about sex and maybe indicate I know a little something about it!

That was just a little story to demonstrate how easily we use labels, but I am writing this to speak into the use of labels. The discussion I was following this morning was about someone calling themselves an alcoholic. On the one hand, when one says they are an alcoholic, this is perceived as negative, and on the other hand as positive. I have a friend who continually refers to himself, privately among those close to him, as a recovering alcoholic. This permits him to remind himself of journey from over thirty years ago. It comes down to a matter of perspective and what helps us help ourselves.

What is dangerous in my mind is the self-talk and the labels we give ourselves, and the labels we may openly give to others. Having worked for more than twenty-eight years with world-renowned psychiatrist Dr. William Glasser, I have become acutely aware of the damaging effects of labels. Think about the DSM5. This is a diagnostic manual for so called psychiatric disorders. If you give anyone a label you are offering them a set of behaviours to live by, according to the DSM5 manual.

I could go on about more labels, but I think the message is clear.

Be careful how you label yourself and others!

I'M IN THE CLOUD!

I have been having e-mail issues so recently I transferred my hosting to the cloud. What in the world is the cloud? As I ponder this, I imagine my e-mails floating overhead somewhere in space! Really, to imagine what this cloud is takes a lot of imagination!

When I think about how far we have advanced technologically in the past two decades, it is incredible! I often think about how my parents would catch me with a tiny transistor radio under my pillow when I went to bed and take it from me because they were afraid I was going to go deaf!

Now I carry my music in my phone and can put an ear bud in my ear and listen to my music at my leisure anywhere I am. It is truly amazing. You know, all of what we have today is a result of someone doing some deep thinking, some imagineering, and making their dreams a reality.

Do you have dreams? Of course you do! You may not even be aware of them. Maybe they are desires or something you really want. What do you tell yourself about your dreams? Are you a naysayer or do you believe your dreams are possible?

Sometimes people say things like "I would love to do or have X, but that will never be me!" Other people will say, "I believe it is possible and I am going to work towards realizing my dream!"

Which type are you? Will you realize your dreams?

Know Your Truth

*"Influence is not making someone conscious of your truth.
It's helping them become conscious of their own."*

– Christian Simpson

This quote is exactly why I love what I do!

My mentor and teacher, Dr. William Glasser, taught me how to become aware of what is happening in my life and to find my own truth or personal power.

He gave the world the gift of understanding total behaviour. All behaviour is total, he said, and all behaviour has four components to it. They are feeling, physiology (body talk), thinking, and acting. At any given time we cannot help how we feel or even what goes on physically in our bodies, but we do have more control over our thoughts and our actions.

Something as simple as wandering around a flea market in the high heat can really be upsetting to a person's body. I did just that this past weekend. I walked for over an hour in 27C temperature and before long I experienced excruciating pain in my back. My body was sending me a signal to pay attention. I felt the pain, my back was weakening, but I was thinking "Just keep going a little further" and I kept pushing along.

You see, I was with my sister-in-law, Carol, who was visiting from Vancouver, and we were having fun! I had my bottle of water and was drinking it to stay hydrated, and we were laughing and carrying on about some of the old stuff we saw! I knew what I was doing. It was more need satisfying to keep pushing along rather than to complain and stop.

Finally though, my back sent a stronger signal to my brain as I felt more and more pain. This time I changed my thinking to "I need to take a little break. We can carry on after I rest a bit, but I need to sit for a few minutes." I told Carol this and she agreed she could use a break too! We saw some benches and sat down.

As we sat quietly on the bench, I asked myself, what is my truth about this flea market? My truth was I didn't need any of the stuff that was for sale, except if I saw some classic children's books for my grandchildren. And Carol couldn't take much of anything back with her since she was flying so why were we doing this to ourselves? With that, we had a chat and decided to leave.

This may sound like a simple solution to noticing pain and relieving it, but some people would never acknowledge what was going on with their body. They'd never accept that they were taxing their body's strength nor would they discuss it with their guest.

In this case, I was conscious of my own truth, but I also wanted to influence Carol who then became conscious of her truth. By the way, we had a fantastic, fun rest of the day, even if it wasn't spent at the flea market.

I Can Make You

Today I received this quote in my e-mail inbox: "How you make others feel about themselves says a lot about you!" As I pondered this quote, I asked myself a couple of questions:

1. *First, can I really make someone feel a certain way?*
2. *Second, if I truly can, then I am very powerful?*

Don't get me wrong. Sometimes we share quotes without thinking a whole lot about what we are saying. If we "make" someone feel bad by the behavior we choose then yes, it says a lot about us.

Here is an idea. We are a society that believes we have that much control over other human beings. Eleanor D. Roosevelt said, "No one can make you feel inferior without your consent!" What did she mean by that? I believe she was suggesting that we alone are responsible for how we feel about anything that happens around us. This is a strong stance to take, but it is so true.

Victor Frankl, while held in the concentration camps during World War II, said that the one thing that they could not control was his mind and his thoughts. When we make statements that indicate that we can actually control someone else's mind, do we really believe that?

What are the implications of Roosevelt's quote? Is there a better way to say it? How about something like: "How others feel when they are with you says a lot about you!" Yes, we can attempt to influence others, but that is about all we can do. Yes, if someone is abusive, we feel miserable and cannot help feeling at that time. But we do have control over what we do. If we choose to internalize it as our truth then, it may feel like they "made" us feel that way.

Even Webster's Dictionary says we can "make someone happy" or "make someone sad." How powerful is that? If I really had that kind of control, I would just make everyone happy!

How about you? What would you choose to do?

People Don't Like To Think

People don't like to think. I know this is a funny statement, but really, when was the last time you took time out to just think? Thinking requires time and energy, and most people don't "think: they need to pause and just... think!

Most folks barely stop to think about their personal visions, goals, and dreams, yet thinking is the necessary work to obtain those dreams. Thinking requires energy. We can think *into* something or we can think *about* something. What is the difference?

To me, thinking *about* something is like a fleeting thought. For example, I saw on Facebook this morning that buildings in downtown Woodstock, NB, were on fire. I thought, "Oh, that is too bad. I hope that everyone got out okay and no one is injured", and then I went about my days' work.

But if I were to really stop and think *into* this event, I might have realized that several people were going to be unemployed, several businesses might be lost to the community, and that there was quite a bit of devastation to this event. It seemed to be an entire block that was on fire with the potential to spread over a great area. This is a huge loss for the community of Woodstock as a whole.

Do we stop and think about our dreams in the same way? Do we plan and organize our thoughts? Do we pay attention to our thinking and any limiting beliefs that may creep in? Do we turn negatives into positives? Thinking is not easy and it takes time.

Will you take the time to pay attention to your thinking? Could something be holding you back from realizing your dreams? How will you know?

Perhaps take some time today and just think about life. After all, aren't you worth it?

PEOPLE CHANGE

When we grow and change, the people around us change. This is a fact that I have been well aware of for many years. Sometimes relationships we have held for periods of even twenty-five years will change. I consider this to be the evolutionary process of relationships.

When you have people in your life that think and believe like you do, life is easy. You gel and generally enjoy each other's company. But what happens when we learn something that truly impacts our life and we start making big changes that help us feel better about ourselves, our work, and life in general?

If you have supportive and caring people in your life, your relationships may, in fact, become stronger. If, however, people in your life are jealous or over-protective and judging you for your behavior, then struggles are inevitable.

It is not so much that we are growing, but that we grow together. So often we grow apart. In today's world, this probably happens more frequently because the universe has opened up to us. Sometimes we see the people we have had in our lives through a different filter.

Recently, I was talking with a friend who has worked hard on herself and has made a lot of changes. She's learned the power of saying "no" more often, and no longer does activities that do not bring her joy or satisfaction. As a result, her partner has chosen to use depressing behaviors.

This is something that totally caught her off guard. Instead of being happy for his significant other, he became afraid of the changes in her and that she would leave. In this case, he was asking for her attention. She recognized that while she was going through these changes she had not shared with him as much as she could have.

Once they had a conversation about it all, he realized that he had some choices to make. He could learn and grow too, he could let go and support her growth, or he could continue to try to control her and their marriage would end.

You see, the quality of a relationship is not about the individuals in the relationship. It is about how each of them focuses and adds to the connection. If, when we grow, we lose sight of what we have between ourselves and our partners, which is basically the core of the relationship, then there will be struggles and it could potentially end.

In your journey of growth, do you remember those important relationships and continue to add to them? If not, what are you going to do about it now?

HOBBIES AS A MEDITATION

Do you have a hobby? This is something I have always made sure I had in my life and I did it naturally. I love basketball and I attend the games whenever I can.

I like to knit, and when I am in the mood, I pick up my knitting needles. The latest craze is coloring. I decided to try it as a means to meditate. Do you ever have trouble quieting your mind?

Do you hear yourself saying, "I don't have time to meditate?" This used to be me until I realized there are times that I naturally meditate — that it is a matter of perspective.

What does meditation mean? The term *meditation* refers to a broad variety of practices that includes techniques designed to promote relaxation, build internal energy or life force.

Think about your hobbies. In today's world we are so caught up in the noise of the internet and external amusements, it could be difficult to calm our minds. I hear over and over again that the most successful people meditate daily. I found that I was telling myself to smarten up until I realized that I meditated daily. It was just in a different form.

Every morning when I wake up, I lay in a contemplative state for about half an hour. I just thought I was being lazy until I actually examined what I was doing during that time. Also, when I am knitting, I am relaxing and building internal energy.

Okay, so basketball may not be so relaxing, but it removes me from my overactive mind and gives me something else to focus on. In each of these cases, if I do one of them daily, it really helps me achieve more.

What about you? What do you do to meditate?

CONSEQUENCES

I was rereading *Conversations with God* recently and was reminded about Dr. William Glasser's teachings about punishment. Since we are now back into the school season and many of you have school aged children, I thought I would share some thoughts and ideas that I have learned from Dr. Glasser.

As a psychiatrist, he developed the Glasser Quality School and did a lot of work in his early years in the Ventura School for Girls. It was a school for young women who had been incarcerated for various crimes. They were difficult to serve and yet he was very successful with them. Why? It was because he did not believe in punishment and allowed these young women to take the natural consequences of their behavior.

A lot of people struggle with this concept. Consequence, simply put, is the natural outcome of a behavior. Yes, we may choose behaviors that both benefit and hurt us, and both have natural outcomes. When we choose the latter, we have already created the natural outcome. What benefit does it give to add punishment or judgment to it?

Punishment is about external control and trying to make someone do something different. I ask you this: "When was the last time someone punished you and you felt good about it?" Can you remember a time when you were punished, told you deserved it, and you bought into that belief? How did you feel about your relationship with that person?

I know. I understand that they were just doing the best that they could at the time with what they knew, but even still, how did you feel about the relationship? Did the punishment bring you closer or push you further apart?

When I think about school and the choices we make, there is always a consequence to them. So when your child chooses not to do their homework, they get reprimanded in school and a note is sent home, ask yourself this question: did they receive the natural consequences of their behavior? How can you, as a parent, help them find more effective behaviors? It is through the process of self-evaluation that your children will decide what is right and what is wrong.

You ask them to evaluate what they could do differently and if they will choose to do that. You could also ask what will the consequences be if they do not keep their commitment.

This is one of the toughest things to do as a parent, especially if you were treated differently by your parents. Empowering your children to make more effective choices will go much further than taking away their favorite video game or cell phone.

A Day For Every Occasion

Happy International Take Care of Yourself Day for everyone! That sounds silly, doesn't it? Does it challenge your thinking? We have a day for every other person or occasion around us, but what about Take Care of Yourself Day?

Does that sound selfish to you? I am all too aware that people do not want to appear self-centered, but I am suggesting that we need to take care of ourselves. If we do not, we will have nothing to give to others.

How many times did you hear while growing up, "Don't be selfish! Share your toys! Stop doing that! That's selfish!" These are all said in a very judgmental tone letting you know that that behavior is wrong. We learn this from our environment and we train our brain not to be selfish.

Then burnout comes along and someone says, "You need to take better care of yourself!" "WHAT? I can't take time for me. Too many people need me!"

First, people around you will be just fine when you take that day for you! Second, to fill yourself up is not selfish. It is to become self-full. You need to fill yourself up if you are going to continue to help others. If we do not do this we will have nothing to give and we will burn out.

As we are growing up we hear that we are selfish. We spend the next several years (or decades) proving to ourselves and others that we are not selfish, sometimes to the point that we become selfless.

So become self-full so you can continue to help others! This is not the same as being selfish!

I vote for an International Take Care of Yourself Day, on a regular, ongoing basis! Do you agree?

A Leap Of Faith

Recently, I hosted another day of Advanced Practicum in Choice Theory, Reality Therapy, and Lead Management. It was a very special day indeed. This group had been together in training for a little over a year and were finally at the end of their training.

I asked them to please share what their experience with the ideas had been since we first met in November. I am not going to tell you what was said, but it became a very profound day as each shared their journey to date.

The reason I write about this is that we must never underestimate the value of relationships. The reason that day became so profound is because we were in a safe place. The first person to speak could not wait to share her news, both good and bad. She set the stage. Each of the others shared their challenges, both personally and professionally.

The real growth began when we used the communication process with each person. When you have an environment conducive to huge personal growth, it is easy for others to share. It needs to be safe, confidential, respectful, and free from fear and judgment.

I remember my only early days of learning these ideas. The growth I experienced was mind-shifting. I made such shifts and changes in my thinking that it was truly profound. It has been this way for the last twenty-eight years.

How can someone continue to teach these ideas for so long you ask? It is because they never get old to me. They become very need satisfying, empowering, and they enable others to take charge of their life.

A Drive To The Past

Today I did something totally out of character for me. I travelled for three hours to simply have lunch with my former nursing classmates. We had a wonderful lunch and chat, and made plans to meet again soon. Three hours later I was back home!

The beauty of this day was that it gave me a chance to drive to the area where I grew up as a child. I had an opportunity for six hours to listen to some educational sessions on my iPod and enjoy some of my favorite music.

It was a beautiful day with the trees and lawns all displaying many shades of green along the winding blue Saint John River. To me, there is no other place in New Brunswick with such a scenic drive.

Sometimes we just need a day like this. The day before I had worked hard producing videos and new information for my website. That evening was all about volunteering for Glasser Canada Board meeting.

Sometimes it is a good thing to take a drive to visit the past. It reminded me of how far I have come since growing up in the small town of Woodstock. It is amazing, really. On one of the educational sessions I was listening to while driving, the speaker was talking about working to your natural talents.

He asked if we are consciously aware of our talents and are we working using them, or are we going to work daily and just going through the motions.

What about you? Are you working to your talents? Are you even aware of your talents?

A WRITER'S STRUGGLE

Some days I struggle to determine what to write about in my daily musings. I begin to focus on the problem of writer's block and the more I focus on the fact that I cannot come up with something to write about, the more frustrated I become! Yesterday I decided to take a look at my own total behavior.

HOW WAS I FEELING?

I was feeling frustrated.

WHAT WAS HAPPENING WITH MY PHYSIOLOGY?

I was starting to get a headache.

WHAT WAS I THINKING?

I can't find anything to write about that makes sense to me.

WHAT WAS I DOING?

Sitting and stewing about the fact I had nothing to write about!

I asked myself to think a little deeper. Was this behavior really helping me? Was there a different way to think about it? What if I just wrote what I was experiencing? So I started to write about the not writing experience. You can see what happened next, can't you?

DOING: I am writing now.
THINKING: I really can write.
FEELING: Silly.
PHYSIOLOGY: Less tension, headache disappearing.

I know better than to go down this road. I have been writing these for over a year now and it is not that difficult, but I needed to bring the *unconscious* into the *conscious!* I needed to do a reality check with me.

This is a prime example of how what we focus on expands. The minute I change my focus, the better things get.

I hope you enjoyed this little trip with me about the struggles of writing. Sometimes we just need to be our own coach and ask ourselves the questions. Of course, there is another way and that is to work directly with a coach. Your choice.

Best Customer Service Ever!

Recently, I had an opportunity to go on a two week cruise to the Caribbean. This cruise was the best vacation ever! My every need was catered to! Cruising is very big business, especially for the cruise line I took my trip on. It inspired me to talk a little about customer service and how it really is all about the relationship between buyer and seller.

We arrived at the seaport of Miami and were greeted right away by porters who gave us a number and took our luggage, telling us it would be outside our room shortly after we boarded the ship. This is a huge benefit to the population travelling on a cruise. It was suggested to us that we head up to the fourteenth floor and have some lunch where a huge buffet waited there for us to enjoy. We had arrived early at the dock so the process would be easier and quicker, so we have ample time to enjoy our meal.

The waiters were amazing, making sure we could find what we needed, everything from cutlery to drinks. After lunch, we made our way to our rooms. Our room attendant was always around, always friendly, and checking to see if we were happy with our cruise.

On one occasion, I met a tour guide outside the ship while we were standing in line waiting to go to buses for a land excursion. They let anyone with a cane or a wheelchair board the bus first. I was standing in line and when I stand a long time my back begins to ache. I said to her "Do you mind if I sit?" She said, "No, not at all." She came and sat with me as another guide came along. I asked her if many people from her community on the island of Barbados worked on the cruise ship to which she replied, "Oh no. It is very difficult to get a job aboard a cruise ship." I found this quite interesting.

As I reflect on that, it takes a very special person to work in those conditions where you are always putting your customer first. In fact, you are going out of your way to see that they are happy. Doing this day in and day out means you are always "on." In talking with some of the workers, I found out that they are hired by contract and that the feedback we give as customers is very important. One of our servers had been on board for eight months. They are also leaving their families behind for long periods as well, yet they seem to love what they do.

I have experienced two cruises now and each one has been the same. I could not imagine being on a cruise ship for a week with unhappy staff. This level of service means the leadership must be incredible as well. The staff is from all parts of the world. I am sure there were conflicts on board, but I was not aware of them.

Being treated this way, I just wanted to add value to them. I had my opportunity to actually name the person and the service I had received when sent an evaluation and feedback form after the cruise.

What are you doing to create positive relationships in your workplace or life? Do you see the benefits?

CALLED OUT IN PUBLIC!

Did you ever experience a time when someone called you names or told you they were dissatisfied with you or something you did? Today I experienced an event where just that happened in a public forum.

You see, this forum is online and is a place where we can talk about events, etc. with our leader. Today was different though. People started talking about how dissatisfied they were with an event without first talking to the leader.

In this forum, three quarters of the people had not even attended the event. One person started speaking and that prompted three or four more to agree with him. Then one person spoke positively about the experience and then another, and another, until the whole thing turned around.

All this reminded me of the time I was working in the operating room and the head nurse became really angry with me and started screaming at me in front of the patients lined up for surgery! What an embarrassing time for me and I felt sorry for the patients. She was upset with me because I took orders from a doctor in the Operating Room who had asked me to bring ALL THE BLOOD for that patient into the room at one time!

When she saw my arms full, she started screaming. We had a rule: one bag at a time, but the doctor was expecting some bleeding and demanded we have extra on hand. The nurse would not listen to me and I chose to ignore her in the best interest of the patient.

She was mad at me all day and all I could think about was how do I resolve this mess. I did not want to scream at her like she did me, so I waited until my day was over and went to ask to speak with her in private. I told her what had happened, how I felt, and what I expected from her in the future.

I dealt with the behavior and I offered a solution. From that day forward I had her respect and she mine.

Have you ever had such an experience? This kind of behavior has the potential to ruin relationships.

It is all about how we choose to confront such issues!

Is Creation An Inside Job?

Sometimes I wonder where ideas come from, but seriously is there really a Creator outside of us? This is a question I am sure that many ponder and the answers are simply accepted as truth.

I remember as a small child questioning the validity of praying to a God somewhere way up in the sky that I could not even see. I had a ton of questions and one day I just stopped asking and accepted it as truth because my parents told me so.

My parents were in my quality world and very need satisfying to me, so I easily adopted their beliefs. I now understand that this was a belief that was handed to me, one that I accepted.

So I woke up thinking about the creator today and I asked myself if the Creator is an inside job or an outside job. For me, it is an inside job. Let me explain.

In my mind, we are created from within right from inception. If we look at it from a purely physiological point of view, it takes a sperm from a man and an ova from a woman, and they have to be joined inside the uterus of the woman to survive. Even insemination and in vitro require the going within.

As a baby, we grow within the uterus until we are ready to be born. Once the life source that is within wants the baby to be born, it is born. As soon as it hits the outside world, it starts to control for what it needs to survive. The baby is born knowing two things: what feels good and what doesn't. It knows how to cry and scream for attention. These are all things that are created within. After a while we learn from our environment and begin to believe we can control the world around us, or someone or something else can have that power over us.

I am not going to continue this discussion, but today I have come to realize that the Creator is really within us. We all have our own inner Creator. This is powerful because in the end we have control over only ourselves and we create the life we are currently experiencing.

CHOOSE FUN

You never know when an interest or hobby will end up taking you places you would never think of going!

A little while ago I saw a woman on Facebook laughing hysterically when she put on her new Chewbacca mask (a Star Wars character). I think this video went viral mostly because of the character and the craziness of the lady.

This woman was having a blast with her new mask. Today I read in the paper that a toy company in Rhode Island made a new Chewy toy with her face on it, invited her to the factory, and gave her the toy!

It says in the paper she has been invited to several events to speak about her post going viral and her love of the character. Imagine! One simple little post in social media has skyrocketed this person to fame!

When we enjoy our life and do what we love amazing things can happen! Fun is one of our very basic needs. We are all born needing some fun in our lives. What have you been doing for fun lately? Do you give yourself permission to have a little fun now and then?

I am encouraging you to stop what you are doing right now and have a little fun. It will make your day brighter and you will feel happier and ready to tackle whatever is in front of you!

About The Author

Maureen Craig McIntosh is known internationally as a Coach, Trainer and Speaker. She has been speaking and training with William Glasser International for the last thirty years as a Senior Faculty Member.

In 2004, Maureen took early retirement as a Public Health Nurse to pursue her dreams of working full-time in her own business as a Canadian Certified Counselor. Two years later she became a Certified Personal and Executive Coach, ACC, and began to grow her coaching practice.

A continual learner, in 2012 Maureen joined the John Maxwell Team where she became a Certified Coach, Trainer, and Speaker. In 2013 she decided to reduce her counseling practice and focus more on Coaching. Today she primarily works as a Coach and Trainer and loves writing her daily musings which she sends to her inner circle. If you would like to receive these musings, visit her website to sign-up:

WWW.MONCTONREALITYTHERAPY.COM

Maureen believes in the value of good relationships and how important they are to our happiness. She is a grandmother of four beautiful grandchildren and enjoys any time she can spend with them. An avid basketball fan, she and her partner hold season tickets for the Moncton Miracles, her local team, in Moncton, New Brunswick, Canada.

www.ingramcontent.com/pod-product-compliance
Lightning Source LLC
Chambersburg PA
CBHW031624040426
42452CB00007B/660